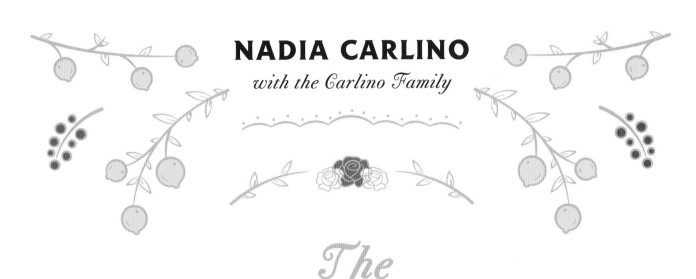

NADIA CARLINO
with the Carlino Family

The CARLINO FAMILY COOKBOOK

Recipes & Stories of Growing Up in a Family
Where Food Brought Us Together

SCHIFFER
PUBLISHING

4880 Lower Valley Road • Atglen, PA 19310

To my family before me who dared to dream,
and to those who made those dreams a reality.

* ❁ *

TO MY GRANDPARENTS:
I am who I am and have all I have today because you both existed.

*Home is not where you are from; it is where you belong. Some of us travel our
whole life to find it. Others find it in a person.*

—Beau Taplin

CONTENTS

PREFACE

In the suburbs of southeastern Pennsylvania, there is a string of communities known as the Main Line. Its neighborhoods account for some of Philadelphia's best places to live. The Main Line got its name from the railroad system that traversed this area in the 1800s, when affluent families built second homes to get away from the city.

No longer a summer-home destination, the Main Line still encompasses many of the most beautiful houses and neighborhoods in the greater Philadelphia area. When we purchased our first home on the Main Line, there weren't many new communities being built, but since then it has seen a booming development that attracts a new generation of residents.

Our family's Italian market, Carlino's, is on the Main Line in the town of Ardmore and is a prominent part of the area's culture. Our store has been around since 1983, created by my grandparents Nicola and Angela Carlino, whom I will introduce in the beginning chapters.

Ardmore is very different now than it was then. It used to be a neighborhood filled with Italians newly emigrated from their hometowns in Italy, where the language was spoken as easily as air flows. Today, only a few Italians remain.

Main Line neighborhoods are filled with lush trees, long driveways, fancy cars, and big dreams. It isn't entirely like that, though, and it would not be the same without every single person who lives there. In fact, our family didn't necessarily fit the mold. Despite that, the Main Line, in all its glory, and sometimes stuffiness, will always be home to me. I will forever love the lush trees overhanging the sidewalks and the long driveways lined with flowers of all varieties.

While it is easy for many to dislike where they were born and raised, sometimes it's nice to romanticize it. Despite its quirks and the fact that I left the state to get away for college, there was nothing quite like the feeling of the train pulling into 30th Street Station in Philadelphia. There's always that little part of your soul that will always register home, whether it's a place or a person. For me, it was both.

I chose to write this book because I wanted to reread it someday and remember all the times I spent in my childhood home and all the recipes shared within it—and of course to invite Carlino's Market's many patrons and longtime friends into our home and family. I wanted to memorialize the house that gave me so much and the people who made that house a home. I felt I could keep my grandparents' memories alive for just a bit longer.

ACKNOWLEDGMENTS

Like most people, I have dreamed of giving an acceptance speech at the Oscars, and this is my chance to imagine what I would say.

The creation of this book would not have been possible without the support of countless people in my life. I want to say a huge thank-you, first to my parents, who were the backbone of this project and helped me from its conception to its completion. There are few words to convey the continued gratitude and love that I feel toward both of you. Thank you to my sister, Angela, for writing and polishing many of the recipes; my brother Nick for believing in my vision and attending meetings with me; and my brother Philip for editing copious drafts of this book and offering helpful insights for recipes and stories. Thank you to my beautiful friends, who kept me sane and rooted for me on days when I needed it most. Thank you to Emma Quinn, whose brilliant photography graces the pages of this cookbook; you genuinely are a rock star, and I am so proud of what we accomplished. Thank you to Cullen Hoppel for designing the beautiful cover and spine; it surpassed my wildest dreams. Thank you to all the silent supporters and angels in the sky who guided my path; I felt you throughout the process, especially on the most-challenging days. Thank you to my lovely editors and the wonderful people at Schiffer Publishing who helped my tiny vision become a reality. Thank you to all the wonderful people at Carlino's whose inspiration, talent, and artistry shine through the pages.

Last, I must thank all the people throughout the years who encouraged me to follow my dreams of being a writer, even when I didn't think it was possible. My younger self and I could not have done it without you.

I am being told to wrap it up via musical interlude by Frank Orman, so let me give a quick shout-out to my Spotify playlist for providing incredible background music and inspiration to write and edit. I could not have done it without you. I did make a playlist for this book, so for readers who wish to listen while you read, my Spotify is ncarlino, and the playlist is called House of Hope.

I am making my way toward the back curtain with the trophy in my hands, and alongside me is the younger version of myself, who only ever dreamt of this moment.

Little Nadia, this one is for you, kid. Glory Be.

This book was written entirely
from my heart, with additional
stories told through the lens
of family members. Through
these stories and food dishes for
entertaining, I hope you will feel
like a part of the Carlino family.

Welcome!

INTRODUCTION

eople often ask me what it was like growing up as a Carlino. Despite what most believe, growing up in my family was like most other people's experiences. Though while some families say a particular family member is the "glue" that holds them together, the glue in my family was food. Food brought us together each day, and it is still what keeps us close. Whether it was our nightly family dinner around our kitchen table or a larger event that somehow always spilled out onto the patio, food was the very thing that never failed to bring everyone together.

It was not until we were ready to move that we realized that this house, our childhood home, wasn't just a house to us. It was a place that held countless memories within every wall and floorboard. It was a place where magic wasn't just imagined; it was created. Each room held different memories for each of us, whether deceased or living. There are so many stories that will never be forgotten.

When we decided to do a second cookbook (our first book was *Wanna Taste? Stories and Recipes from Mama Carlino's Kitchen*), I looked back on my previous writings and found a rough outline for this one. I had written the outline just as I was getting ready to leave for college and just before the house was going up for sale. I remember I wanted to do everything in my power to ensure that this home, the home where I learned to ride a bike and swim, and cooked with my grandmother, was remembered. It was never just a house to me; it had a heartbeat. Saying goodbye to your childhood home is like saying goodbye to an old friend that you know you will see occasionally, but it will never feel the same because too much time has passed. But you'll never forget the fond memories you made together. This home was an old friend, and friends deserve a proper send-off.

Our house played a critical part in our upbringing, which is why this book is centered on it. When my parents first purchased that home, it was a one-story rancher with a sizable backyard. After many years, they built a second addition to fit all of us comfortably. The house's outdoor walls were a lovely peach, and the roof was light gray. It was surrounded by lush trees and had the same distinctive brick features. The driveway ended with a black gate that was never closed, and a black mailbox with lettering in vibrant white.

When I revisit the house, the trees are still lush and the walls are still peach. The shingles are black with a touch of white to highlight the corners of the house. The black gate is now closed, though the mailbox looks the same. While that house is no longer ours, it is still deeply loved.

Our family made this house a home filled with laughter. There was so much love wrapped around every corner and nestled within every cushion—so much that one could never be unsure of it. I know I was lucky, and I still am.

There are four children in our family, plus our parents, Pat and Laura, and our grandparents, who are no longer with us. At one point, there were eight of us living in the house. While that may seem too many for some, I never felt more comfortable. With more people came more stories, more food, and, of course, more love. With that said, I will introduce you to my family in the best way that I can. Every family member is made up of their own beautiful chaos and has a particular food that I associate with them.

Meet the Family

Let's begin with my grandparents Angela and Nicola, who started Carlino's Market with my parents. Countless recipes still made today were passed down from my great-grandparents and beyond. For those who do not know my grandparents' story, I will tell it short and sweet, like a ricotta cannoli.

My grandparents were born and raised on family farms in the small town of Casoli, Italy. They met and fell in love at a young age, and when they were old enough to legally marry, they eloped. In 1968, after nearly fourteen years of marriage, my grandparents decided that they wanted more out of their lives and for their children. They left everything and everyone they knew and loved to come to America.

Back then, going to a new country meant that you didn't know if you would ever see your family again, let alone the place you grew up, so their send-off was more like a funeral than a goodbye party. They weren't just grieving for their relatives and the town; they were grieving the life they knew.

My grandfather's brother, Philip, and his wife, Betty, sponsored my grandparents and their children to come to America. They have told countless stories of their boat voyage to Ellis Island. Although my dad arrived a few years after his Uncle Frank, they have the same memory of the incredibly early morning when they could finally spot Ellis Island and the port of New York. The sun was just barely grazing the horizon, and people on the boat were screaming with joy that they had made it to America. This was their chance to have the life they'd always wanted.

My dad was six years old when he arrived, and my mom was nine when her family made the trip. Their impressions of those first years were similar in some cases but different in others. My dad can still recall some traumatizing encounters with peers, name-calling, ethnocentrism, and more. On the other hand, my mom had many teachers and peers who wanted to help her transition to America. One explanation for their differing experiences could be that my dad had not attended school in Italy, while my mom completed kindergarten through third grade.

Trying to assimilate into a new culture is not easy for anyone. Many of the ingrained Italian customs and traditions are still heavily present in our family. One of those traditions is having your parents or in-laws live with you.

My grandparents lived with us from the beginning, and my grandmother was influential in the choice of our childhood home. Angela was a very religious person; she started and ended every day by either saying a rosary or praying to Padre Pio. For years, she would pass the house on her way to work as a seamstress and cleaning lady before opening the store, and she would say, "What a beautiful house. I wish that one day I could live in a house like that." Every day, without fail, she essentially manifested that house for herself without even being aware of it.

When the house finally came on the market, my dad took my grandparents and mom to the Sunday open house. When they toured the rancher, they were absolutely in awe, because they had never imagined being able to live in a place of that size. My mom looked at my dad and said she was in love with it, but there was no way they could ever afford it. But that's the funny thing about life: when you least expect it, beautiful things happen. Especially when you work as hard as they did and still do.

Weeks later, my parents took my grandparents to the house again and told them it was ours now. My grandmother was at a loss for words. The house she had always wished for had become hers.

One of the main reasons my grandmother loved that house was not just for its aesthetically pleasing nature or its beautiful location, but because it sat next door to a retreat center. The St. Raphaela Center was my grandmother's vision of peace, and that home was her House of Hope. After my parents purchased the house, they created a direct path to the retreat center so

Mama and Pop Carlino with my Uncle Carmen (left) and my dad (right) at their house in Italy

that my grandmother could walk there daily after work to pray. That path became her haven, and it is one that I sometimes still walk just to imagine that she is walking with me.

My grandfather loved the house for other reasons, particularly for its abundance of land and good exposure to the sun so he could grow his flowers and vegetable garden. He planted a fig tree in the side yard and a beautiful tomato and herb garden in the back. In front of the house, he planted flowers of all kinds, and in colors that never failed to make people smile as they passed. My grandfather took pride in the beauty he created, both in the house and outside it.

When I think back to that time, I can still hear my grandparents' footsteps coming down the hallway and the sweet smell of fresh basil in the kitchen. My grandparents were so significant to my upbringing that leaving that house felt like leaving a piece of them with it. All those memories would come with me, good and sometimes sad, but the rooms in which they took place will forever stand still in time, like a Polaroid collecting dust.

Though each family member has a dish that I associate with them, I cannot choose one for my grandparents. It is like deciding which flowers are the most beautiful when you are in a field in full bloom.

My grandparents forever live in my family's memories and minds. We will never forget everything they have given us and everything they gave up to achieve their legacy. Everything we do is because of their sacrifices to ensure that we never lacked anything. They also happened to provide the world with two beautiful children, one of whom I am lucky enough to call Dad.

Carmen Carlino, Buonanima (Good Soul)

My grandparents brought two incredible sons into the world, and they have made this family what it is. My Uncle Carmen was older than my dad, but they were exceptionally close.

Growing up, my uncle was different than most people. It was as if he had no worries or reservations about life, or at least he never showed it. It was like he knew the secret to life before anyone else did. My dad always told me that my uncle would smile constantly and laugh deeply. He said it was like my uncle knew his life would end before anyone wanted it to.

When Uncle Carmen was thirty-three, he passed away in a tragic accident. The life that once was filled with so much laughter and love and exuberance was gone. That day, the world as we knew it went dark. Though my brother Philip and I weren't born yet, I still feel as if we were there, just from hearing my family talk about him and his untimely passing.

Despite never knowing my Uncle Carmen, I find myself missing him much more than anyone would expect. Some days I even believe I can hear his deep belly laugh or see his face in those of strangers. Some days, I feel I knew him in another life. I will forever wish I could have met him.

While there is no proper way to describe the insurmountable loss of someone as immensely loved as Carmen, I strive to keep his memory alive for my grandparents and parents. Uncle Carmen, you are and forever will be one of the most beautiful parts of our story, and we will never forget you.

I now know that the secret to life is living each day as if it could be gone tomorrow. Because it could, and it did.

Uncle Carmen (*left*) and my dad at the original Ardmore store

Pasquale Carlino

The other beautiful child that my grandparents brought into the world was my dad, Pasquale, or Pat, as he is called. My dad is unlike what most people expect when they first look at him. He looks solemn, and many people find him intimidating. However, he is a giant teddy bear with a heart of liquid gold.

My dad is a generous human being and has one of the kindest souls of anyone I have encountered. He always feels as if he could do more for someone, even if he's done everything he could. My dad would give up everything to ensure that the people he loves are okay.

Along with his kind heart, he has the funniest facial expressions and the best sense of humor. I say that because I am one of the only people who consistently gets his jokes and laughs at them. That is another reason we get along so well.

Few people get to see my dad the way that I do, though. Those moments where he is utterly content staring at deer in the backyard or inhaling the refreshing smell of the outdoors. The moments when his eyes light up when he sees his grandchildren, or the way his voice softens when he feels particularly loved.

Despite our past difficulties due to teenage angst and the devastating effects of grief, our relationship has only gotten stronger. My dad is my biggest supporter and fan. He drove three hours in a terrible windstorm to pick me up from college, despite many others turning around and driving back home. Some may call that a death wish; I call it the truest expression of acts of service. My dad also

wrote and texted me daily motivational quotes when I was finishing college online during the pandemic, and he still does today.

There are not enough words in the English language to describe how much he means to me, and I will search my entire life until I find them. When I think of my dad, I think of the concoctions he creates for dinner almost every night when he asks us what we want, and we respond with "I don't know." One dish he created that we love is pasta with zucchini. This recipe is like my dad: warm and comforting, with just the right amount of randomness.

ZUCCHINI PASTA IN WHITE WINE SAUCE

PREPARATION

1. Heat a large skillet over medium-high heat. Add the olive oil and garlic and sauté until the garlic is golden brown. Remove the garlic and add the onions, cooking until they are golden in color. Add the white wine and simmer until most of the wine is reduced.

2. Add the grape tomatoes and sauté for about 4 minutes. Add the zucchini and lemon juice and sauté until the zucchini is tender.

3. Bring a pot of salted water to a boil. Cook Gemelli or your pasta of choice as directed until al dente.

4. Drain the pasta, reserving 1 cup of the pasta water.

5. Add the pasta and reserved pasta water to the skillet. Stir all together. Top with fresh Parmigiano-Reggiano, and lemon zest, and stir. Simmer for another minute or two, garnish with the parsley, and enjoy!

Serves 2

INGREDIENTS

6 tablespoons olive oil

4 garlic cloves, cut in half

1 small Vidalia onion, chopped

½ cup white wine
(preferably a good Pinot Grigio)

2 large zucchinis, sliced

juice of **1** lemon

24 grape tomatoes, halved

2 teaspoons salt

1 pound Gemelli pasta

1 tablespoon lemon zest

black pepper to taste

¼ cup Parmigiano Reggiano

¼ cup basil, roughly chopped

Laura DiNardo Carlino

Luckily for my siblings and me, my dad married a pretty great woman. She is known to some as Laura or Mrs. C., but I know her as Momma or Mom. My mom is the definition of chaotic good. She will go above and beyond for anyone she loves, but she will also not tolerate any nonsense. She would use a different word, so use your imagination.

Many employees know my mom in all her graces, but to many, she is not just their boss but their work mom. Many who have worked at the stores for a while call her Mrs. C., which is their way of saying Mom. That is just who she is. My mom will always ensure that everyone is fed and cared for, while also ensuring that the stores are stocked and everything is as it should be.

While my mom sometimes has a flair for dramatics and her temper can be a ticking time bomb, she also has the biggest heart of anyone I know. She holds so much love within her that a simple touch could heal even the most broken of souls.

After long hours of work and the increasing aches in her hands and feet from arthritis, she still manages to make our house a home and listen to my nonsensical ramblings. She makes time to watch her grandchildren weekly and ensures the bills are paid on time. Despite the obstacles in her path, she still manages to get up every morning and give herself to the world and her family.

One example of her love is the number of times a day I would call her when I was in college. I just needed to hear her voice. On record, it was about two times a day; off record, it was close to three or four. I spent many

nights with my parents on speaker while they ate dinner at home, and I ate in my dorm room before studying so I could feel like they were there. My mom is the very definition of home.

One of the recipes she created and that we all adore is tomato sauce with fresh sausage over homemade pasta. Every time I came home on college breaks, she knew what to make first. I knew I was finally home when we would all sit down around the kitchen table with our steaming pasta bowls.

TOMATO SAUCE *with* SAUSAGE

PREPARATION

1. Place the whole tomatoes in a mixing bowl. Using your hands, gently crush the tomatoes until they form even chunks. Set aside.

2. In a large sauté pan over medium heat, cook the sausage in the olive oil until half browned and add the diced onion. Sauté until the onions are golden in color.

3. Add the crushed tomatoes and juice to the pan of cooked sausage. Add salt and pepper to taste. While stirring, bring to a boil. Lower the heat and stir occasionally so that the mixture doesn't stick. Simmer for 30 minutes. Add the basil and Parmigiano Reggiano to taste. Simmer for 5 minutes.

4. Pair this sauce with your favorite penne, rigatoni, or pappardelle pasta.

Serves 4-6

INGREDIENTS

3 28-ounce cans whole peeled tomatoes (preferably San Marzano)

1½ pounds fresh Italian sausage, casings removed (hot or sweet, or combination of both)

6 tablespoons olive oil

1 large, sweet onion, diced

salt and pepper to taste

6 leaves fresh basil, chiffonade

⅓ cup grated Parmigiano Reggiano

Angela Carlino Milani

The oldest of my siblings is Angela Milani, or Ang, as we call her. Although we are twelve years apart in age, she has always made me feel like I was as important to her as any of her friends, which is rare for someone in high school and later college. Ang was more of a mother to me than a sister. She would often change my diapers as a baby, brush my hair, play with me when I was a toddler, and take me to lunch and buy me clothes when I was a teenager.

Honestly, there were times when I wished she was more of a sister to me than a mother, but as I have grown, I have realized what a blessing it was to have someone who constantly put me first when she didn't have to. Oldest siblings, especially the oldest daughters, do not receive the credit they deserve, so thank you, Ang.

To many, my sister is the level-headed, creative genius in the stores. To me, she is Mary Poppins and Superwoman combined into one. Anytime I see her, no matter what kind of day she is having, she has a smile on her face and a twinkle in her eyes. I greatly admire that about her.

Ang is Superwoman and Mary Poppins because she manages to care for three children under age nine while also being the chief operating officer of two stores. She regularly attends their sports games, makes pickups from school, puts together school events, keeps the house organized, and feeds her family. This does not leave much time for her to take care of herself, but she rarely complains. As Chef Angela, she was the face of Carlino's before she had to loosen the reins when she was expecting her first child.

Whenever I think of my sister and food, I think of eggplant parmigiana. If there is one thing my sister loves, it's our eggplant parm, and often, after a long day, it can put a smile on her face like no other dish! She is a simple woman: the way to her heart is through her stomach, and eggplant parm or eggplant meatballs are the key.

POLPETTE *Di* MELANZANE

PREPARATION

1. Preheat the oven to 350 degrees and place the rack on the middle level.

2. Cube the eggplant into 1" pieces. Crush and make a paste of the garlic cloves. Rough-chop the basil leaves. Set aside.

3. In a large pan on medium-low heat, sauté garlic in the olive oil. After 2 minutes, add the eggplant and mix thoroughly. Add the water to the pan, cover, and let cook for 20 minutes.

4. Turn off the heat and move the softened eggplant to a large mixing bowl. Let the eggplant cool for a few minutes, then add the bread crumbs, Pecorino Romano, pepper, basil, and eggs. Mix well.

5. With wet hands, form the eggplant mixture into balls the size of a baseball. Push one piece of mozzarella into the center of each ball, close the hole, and place on a sheet pan lined with parchment paper. Bake for 25–30 minutes until golden brown.

6. Simmer the eggplant balls for about 10 minutes in your favorite fresh tomato sauce, and serve hot.

NOTES

Unseasoned bread crumbs are recommended to let the basil and cheese shine through.

Use any type of firm, fresh eggplant.

Make sure the eggplant isn't too hot before adding the egg, cheese, and remaining ingredients.

Roll the eggplant meatballs with wet or oiled hands to avoid sticking.

No extra salt was added due to the inherent saltiness of Pecorino Romano cheese.

Makes enough to simmer the polpette and extra for pasta

INGREDIENTS

6 medium eggplants

1 cup basil leaves

4 garlic cloves, chopped

½ cup extra-virgin olive oil

½ cup water

3 cups bread crumbs

1½ cup Pecorino Romano cheese

2 teaspoons black pepper

4 large eggs, beaten

8 ounces fresh mozzarella, cubed

TOMATO BASIL SAUCE

Makes 8 quarts

INGREDIENTS

2 28-ounce cans of whole peeled tomatoes

¼ cup extra-virgin olive oil

4 cloves garlic, minced

half an onion

1 28-ounce can pureed tomatoes

1 cup water

salt and pepper to taste

red pepper flakes (optional)

1 bunch fresh basil, roughly chopped

PREPARATION

1. Pour whole tomatoes into a small bowl and lightly crush with your hands to form chunks. Set aside.

2. Heat the olive oil in a large saucepan over medium heat. Add the garlic and onion, stirring until browned.

3. Add the crushed tomatoes, pureed tomatoes, water, salt, pepper, and red pepper flakes to the pan. Cook on medium heat, stirring occasionally until the sauce comes to a boil and thickens.

4. After 30–35 minutes, add the basil, leaving a whole leaf or two for presentation, and turn off the heat.

5. Plate the sauce with your eggplant polpette or pasta of choice.

Nick Carlino

My brother Nick Carlino, or Nicky as we know him, is my older brother. Nick is the mastermind behind most of the marketing in both stores and can be seen in either location daily.

I loved spending time with Nicky as a child. Whenever Nick laughs, you are bound to laugh with him. He also has impeccable style and an eye for beauty in all its forms. Growing up, he would take me shopping and buy me things I did not need, but gift-giving is his love language, and who was I to discourage that? Nick is also an extremely hard worker and genuinely wants to enjoy life in all its facets and quirks. He has a dog named Lilly, who is like his child; she is my favorite excuse to go over and bother him.

Nick is the kind of person that you could say, "Let's get a milkshake and fries and tell no one," and you know he would not tell a soul. He is also the kind of person who will make you feel incredibly loved while reminding you that he worked hard to ensure that you felt it.

In another life, Nick would be a great luxury car salesman or someone who gets paid to rate their experience in hotels. He was meant for the finer things in life, and I hope he knows that he is the most important gift any of us could have received.

When I think of my brother Nicky, I think of cheesecake. His favorite guilty pleasure food is our ricotta cheesecake with Amarena cherries. It is just like him: sweet, fruity, and hard to say no to.

RICOTTA CHEESECAKE
with AMARENA CHERRIES

Serves 8

INGREDIENTS

4 cups ricotta, preferably impastata
dry ricotta

softened butter and dry, fine bread
crumbs for the pan

6 large eggs, separated

pinch of salt

¾ cup sugar

zest of **1** large orange

½ cup heavy cream

Amarena cherries

PREPARATION

1. If you are using regular ricotta cheese, place the ricotta in a sieve lined with a cheesecloth, and place the sieve over a bowl. Cover the ricotta tightly with plastic wrap and place it in the refrigerator for at least 8 hours or up to a day. If you are using ricotta impastata, you can skip this step.

2. Preheat the oven to 375 degrees.

3. Lightly coat an 8" springform pan with softened butter, then sprinkle bread crumbs over the butter generously to cover it. Shake out excess crumbs.

4. Using a whisk attachment on a stand mixer, beat the egg yolks, sugar, and salt until fully combined. Add the drained ricotta and orange zest. Continue to whisk until the ingredients are incorporated, then beat in the heavy cream.

5. In a separate bowl, using a hand mixer or whisk, beat the egg whites until they form peaks when the beater is lifted from the mixture.

6. Gently stir in about a third of the egg whites to the ricotta mixture, using a spatula or spoon, then fold in the remaining egg whites.

7. Pour the cake mixture into the springform pan and bake until the cake reaches a golden-brown color and is set in the center, about 1 hour and 10 minutes.

8. Allow the cake to cool completely before removing the sides of the pan.

9. Top the cheesecake with Amarena cherries or dust with powdered sugar.

Philip Carlino

My second-oldest brother is Philip, or Phil. Not many people have the pleasure of meeting Phil because he works remotely on the back end of the business. He loves planting, spending time outdoors, and enjoying nature with a good book. Phil is one of the most intelligent people I know, and he also happens to be one of my favorite people in the world. Wherever Philip is, I am sure to be close behind, whether it is a car ride or a walk around the neighborhood.

Since we were children, I wanted to be like my big brother Philip. I would even steal his T-shirts and his favorite number. There is only a four-year age difference between us, which has made it easy for us to get along.

When my mom was expecting me and had extreme morning sickness, Phil would rub her belly and try to help as best as a four-year-old could, because that is just the kind of soul he has. After I was born, he would not stray far from me, either. It was as if we were attached even then.

As we got older and went our separate ways, we made sure never to lose touch, whether it was a simple text or a mindless tweet that we knew would make the other smile. Phil is one of my best friends and never fails to make me feel beautiful and intelligent. He reminds me that I have much to offer this world, especially when I forget.

When I told him that I was writing this book, he reminded me that I was "a genius with a Mensa IQ." That is not true, but he sure as heck made me believe it. Phil sets a high bar for the people in my life, for which I am grateful.

When Phil began to struggle with food sensitivities, he adopted a gluten-free and dairy-free diet. Through his experience, I also became dairy-free. Phil began to

develop new recipes from our family's old traditions so that he could eat the foods he loved without getting sick. His recipes are so delicious that we all enjoy eating them, despite the many alterations.

Recently, my brother created a gluten-free, dairy-free meatball recipe that is simply delightful and very easy to make. When I think of him, I think of so many wonderful childhood memories, but also of these meatballs.

DAIRY-FREE & GLUTEN-FREE MEATBALLS

Serves 6-8

INGREDIENTS

1 pound ground beef

1 pound ground pork

1 pound ground veal

1 egg

½ yellow onion, small dice

2 cloves garlic, minced (optional)

6 leaves basil, chiffonade

2 teaspoons kosher salt

1 teaspoons ground black pepper

2 cups gluten-free panko bread crumbs, unseasoned

1 **24**-ounce jar Carlino's Marinara Sauce

PREPARATION

1. Preheat oven to 375 degrees.

2. In a large bowl, add all three types of ground meat. Mix the meat with your hands and create a well in the center.

3. Add the egg, onion, garlic, and seasonings and thoroughly combine with your hands. Add bread crumbs and continue mixing until combined.

4. Using your hands, roll the meat into balls about the size of a golf ball. Place them on a parchment-lined baking sheet and bake for 30–40 minutes.

5. Add the meatballs and Carlino's Marinara Sauce to a saucepan and simmer for 20 minutes. Then, serve the meatballs and sauce with roasted spaghetti squash or your favorite gluten-free pasta.

Nadia Carlino

I came last in the family lineup. To some, I am Nad or Nads; to my grandfather, I was *la stella piu bella del mondo*, or the most beautiful star in the world. To my family, I am the child who they are unsure of where I came from.

I graduated from college amid the pandemic in 2021 with a degree in psychology and anthropology. After graduating, I felt like Nicole Kidman after her divorce from Tom Cruise. If you don't understand, google it. The first image that pops up of Nicole is a national treasure.

Many people have asked what I was going to do with my life when I finished school. I did not have an answer, at least not one that I thought they wanted to hear. Simply put, I wanted to be happy. I wanted to see the world. I wanted to take a long pause before going back to school or working for the rest of my life. I wanted to live freely for just a bit longer.

My desire since high school has been to write this book, and with the newfound free time after graduating, I decided that there was no better time than the present. While I cannot describe myself through my family's eyes, I can undoubtedly say that my family would not be complete without me.

In the last book, ten-year-old me said I wanted to be the main chef like my grandmother. While that dream has changed, one thing remains. Every day, I strive to make my grandmother proud in whatever capacity I can. Without my grandparents' vision for a better life in America, my siblings and I would not be where we are today. I am forever grateful for their sacrifices, and those of my parents, to ensure that my siblings and I had a better life than they did.

My grandmother always told us to work from our heart or don't do anything at all. Through this book, I hope you will begin to understand who we are when the store is closed and the lights are turned off.

When I think of growing up in our beautiful home, one particular evening comes to mind. My parents were working late, and I had school the following day, so my grandmother cooked my favorite meal: cheese ravioli with marinara sauce. Despite its simplicity, it was everything that went along with it that made it my favorite. I can vividly picture it now.

After my grandmother cooked the pasta and we dished it out, my grandfather sat with his back against the foot of the couch, and my grandmother sat in her rocking chair toward the hall near the kitchen. I sat between in a world entirely my own. Once we sat down, the news played softly in the background like a lullaby, and I felt what I can only describe as serenity. It was a feeling that I do not feel very often now.

That night, I decided to put red pepper flakes on my ravioli like my grandparents did, and my grandfather was so proud of me that I could not help but beam with pride. It was just the three of us, which was exceedingly rare. That night, it was just us, and the world was quiet.

It was the most mundane of evenings. Yet, it is one memory that has stayed with me. In moments like that one, I feel I knew what true happiness was. For a moment when I reminisce about it, the part of me that is not nostalgic or misty eyed is living within that child, at that moment where she felt truly free.

DAIRY-FREE RAVIOLI ALLA POMODORO
Pasta Sheets

Serves 4-6

INGREDIENTS

2 cups all-purpose flour, or more as needed

1 teaspoon kosher salt

3 large eggs

2 large egg yolks

1 teaspoon olive oil

PREPARATION

1. On a large wooden surface, combine flour and salt in a large bowl and make a well in the middle. Using a fork, gradually mix in the egg yolks and olive oil until clumps begin to form.

2. When the mixture becomes too difficult to stir with a fork, use your hands. Sprinkle some extra flour on the board and knead the dough until it is quite stiff and no longer sticky. Transfer the dough to a bowl and cover with plastic or a cloth, and let it rest for about 30 minutes.

3. Lightly sprinkle the wooden board with flour. Cut off a fourth of the dough; keep the rest covered while you work.

Roll the dough in flour, then flatten it into a rectangle about the width of your hand. Using a rolling pin, roll over the dough up and down, left and right. Flip the dough about every two dozen rolls. If the dough sticks, dust it with more flour. Repeat until the pasta is roughly 24" long and 8" wide. Dust with flour and set aside; repeat with the remaining dough. The pasta sheet should be thin enough to see your hand through it.

4. To form jackets for the ravioli, cut each sheet of dough into rectangles about 24" long and 4" wide, trimming the edges neatly.

VEGAN RICOTTA FILLING

PREPARATION

1. Place the cashews in purified water in a bowl overnight, then drain the cashews. Set aside.

2. Bring water to a boil in a small saucepan over medium-high heat and add the almonds. Boil for one minute and then remove them from the heat and drain them. This will allow the skins to fall off. You can also buy preprepared raw almonds and cashews if you wish to skip this step.

3. Combine the cashews, almonds, lemon juice, and nutritional yeast in a blender. Blend until the mixture has a uniform texture. If the mixture is on the drier side and not blending properly, add a dash or two of water until it becomes smooth.

4. Place the mixture in a piece of cheesecloth placed in a bowl, band it with a string, and refrigerate overnight.

ASSEMBLY

1. Spread the vegan ricotta in the center of the pasta dough about 1" thick.

2. Fold the sheet over and close the edges of the ravioli with beaten egg, then paint it on with a pastry brush. When the edges are closed, press down with a fork to seal.

3. Bring a medium pot of salted water to a boil, while you bring your sauce to a simmer (see page 15). Place the ravioli in the boiling water until they float to the top. Once they are cooked, drain the water, add the ravioli to the sauce, and enjoy!

Serves 4

INGREDIENTS

1 cup raw cashews

1 cup raw almonds

juice from half a lemon

nutritional yeast to taste

salt and pepper to taste

Home is the nicest word there is.

—LAURA INGALLS WILDER

1993

In 1993, my grandmother's dream house had become ours. After slowly unpacking kitchen utensils and limited cooking supplies, my grandparents and parents prepared a small feast to celebrate their new reality. Though the house was relatively empty, the joy and possibilities for the future made the place feel full. Only my older siblings Ang and Nick were on the scene at the time; Philip and I had yet to be born. My family would live there until we sold the house in 2017.

Ang and Nick ran through the house in awe. They had never known such a spacious home. My parents and grandparents, too, were accustomed to cramped living spaces where beds were often shared with siblings. This house was truly a place of dreams and hope.

For dinner that evening, my family decided to stick to something on the simpler side. My dad and grandfather had prepared homemade grappa in advance, a classic Italian drink consisting of what is left of the grapes used to make wine. In olden times, grappa was known as the water of life or *aqua vitae*. Today, grappa and *aqua vitae* are considered two different forms of fermented drinks. Regardless, grappa is Italy's version of brandy, with a bold and flavorful taste that packs a punch.

My grandmother prepared a lovely frittata as a side, and my mom made her now-famous (in my household) pan-roasted lemon and herb chicken. While it was simple, the meal was important because it would be the first of many in this new house.

Our house, 1993

FRITTATA WITH POTATO, ONION & ROSEMARY

Serves 4–6

INGREDIENTS

2 tablespoons olive oil

2 large potatoes, peeled and sliced thick

3 yellow bell peppers, thinly sliced

6 eggs, beaten

1 medium onion, thinly sliced

2 sprigs fresh rosemary, stems removed

salt and pepper to taste

PREPARATION

1. Heat oil in a large skillet or frying pan over medium-high heat. Spread the potato slices on the bottom of the pan with the onions and cook, turning once, until the potatoes are golden on both sides.

2. In a separate small skillet over medium heat, sauté the bell peppers in 2 tablespoons of olive oil until they are soft, about 8 minutes.

3. Turn the heat to high. Pour the beaten eggs into the pan and season with salt and pepper and rosemary. Tilt the pan so that the eggs spread across the bottom of the pan. Turn the heat to medium low and cook for 15–20 minutes.

4. Cover the pan with a plate and flip the pan to turn the frittata onto the plate. Slide the frittata back into the pan with the uncooked side down. Cover and let cook for another 4–5 minutes.

5. Transfer the frittata to a serving dish, top with the sautéed peppers, and garnish with lemon and parsley.

LEMON & HERB ROASTED CHICKEN

PREPARATION

1. Rinse the chicken well and pat dry with a paper towel; season both sides of the thighs with ground pepper and salt.

2. In a heavy skillet, add olive oil and heat on medium high. Place the chicken in the skillet and add garlic, thyme, red pepper flakes, and paprika.

3. Cook each side until golden brown and slightly sticking to the pan, roughly 15 minutes on each side or until the internal temperature reaches 165 degrees. Add the lemon zest and juice and remove from the heat.

4. Transfer to a serving dish and add thinly sliced lemons and fresh parsley for garnish

Pictured on page 28

Serves 4–6

INGREDIENTS

2½ pounds bone-in, skin-on chicken thighs

⅓ cup olive oil

3 cloves garlic, minced

2 sprigs fresh thyme

½ teaspoon paprika

⅓ teaspoon crushed red pepper flakes

zest and juice of **2** large lemons

1 large onion, peeled and quartered

1 lemon, thinly sliced for garnish

Fresh parsley, chopped, for garnish

salt and fresh black pepper to taste

GRAPPA COCKTAIL

Grappa is an after-dinner drink otherwise known as a *digestivo*. Espresso is also traditionally consumed after dinner, so a combination of the two is a match made in heaven. Italian law specifies that any drink called grappa must be produced in Italy. If you want the real thing, buy an Italian bottle.

INGREDIENTS

⅔ ounce Italian grappa
1 shot of espresso
half a shot of amaretto, or **0.5** ounces
grated nutmeg

PREPARATION

Shake the grappa, espresso, and amaretto over ice and pour into a cup. A splash of milk can be added for a creamier flavor. Almond milk brings out the flavor of the amaretto. Add grated nutmeg on top.

1995

My mom became quite sick shortly after settling into the new house. It was not the usual stomach bug or cold, or even allergies; it was the joy of pregnancy. In late 1994, my mom was expecting Philip, and the excitement was enough to fuel a small town.

My mom suffered from persistent nausea throughout all her pregnancies, but that didn't stop her from working. Throughout the day, she would drink chamomile tea and brodo, or broth. Sometimes, pasta can be put into the broth to create pastina, or it can simply be sipped as is. It is quite literally liquid gold to most Italians, and for my mom, it was God-sent at the time.

Philip was born in the early evening of July 11, 1995. He was the largest of her babies, which resulted in a complicated birth. Overall, though, it was an enormous success: After my dad cut the umbilical cord and held Phil for the first time, Phil smiled at him. And then Phil peed on him. My dad remembers that night as one of the happiest of his life.

In Italian culture, it is customary to bring a new mom Italian wedding soup. However, my mom continued to drink plain broth, even when my grandmother offered to make whatever she wanted.

When my dad told my siblings and grandparents that Philip had been born, they were so excited that they could hardly wait to meet him, and when they did, it was love at first sight. Philip's middle name, Gabriel, was selected because of San Gabriele, whose central shrine is in Abruzzo, Italy, where my family is from. When my mom was sick during her pregnancy, she would pray to St. Gabriel for strength, guidance, and perseverance, so she felt it was fitting that it would be Philip's middle name.

His first name comes from my grandfather's brother, Philip Carlino, one of the first of the family to emigrate from Italy. When my family first came to America, they stayed with my Uncle Philip and his wife, Aunt Betty, who were their sponsors. A few months before my family came to America, Uncle Philip and Aunt Betty lost their only son, who was three. Despite their heartache, Uncle

My mom, Nicky, and my sister, Angela, holding a newborn Philip at the hospital

Philip and Aunt Betty welcomed my grandparents and their two young sons and helped them make their start in a new country.

When my parents chose the name Philip, my dad wanted to be the first to tell them. As he recalls, Uncle Philip and Aunt Betty were standing in the kitchen when he arrived, and were happy to hear that the baby was healthy. My dad told them to sit down, and then he looked at my uncle and said, "We named the baby Philip after you." At that moment, Aunt Betty started to cry. It was the first time my dad had ever seen her cry. And my uncle was elated.

When my parents took my brother to see his new namesake, they put him into Aunt Betty's arms, and she looked at him as if he was baby Jesus. Her heart was so filled with love and joy that she did not want to put him down. At that moment, all was right in the world again.

Growing up, Philip ate a lot of pasta and bread. When his stomach became sensitive, pasta brought more pain than comfort. Mom and Dad would make him dishes with no pasta, sauce, or heavy spices such as garlic, which often helped.

Once he was old enough to start cooking, Philip began experimenting with dairy-free and gluten-free alternatives, including meatballs and pork shoulder with apples. Another classic dish that Philip enjoyed before his health decline was good ol' apple pie with ice cream. So that Phil could continue to enjoy his favorite childhood dish, I developed a recipe for a gluten-free apple crostata, which follows.

TRADITIONAL BRODO *with* PASTINA

Serves 2

INGREDIENTS

32 ounces homemade bone broth (recipe on page 33)

½ cup frozen mixed vegetables or fresh mixed vegetables

fresh basil leaves, whole

gluten-free pastina of choice

seasoning to taste

PREPARATION

1. Place the bone broth into a small saucepan. Add a dash of water if the taste is too strong for your liking.

2. When the broth comes to a slow, rolling boil, add the vegetables and stir occasionally.

3. Add the pastina and cook as directed on the package, stirring occasionally.

4. When all the contents in the pot are cooked thoroughly, add fresh basil leaves and season to taste. Put into a bowl and serve.

NOTE
Bone broth is typically salted unless the package indicates otherwise.

Aunt Betty, Philip, and Uncle Phillip at our house for a birthday party

HOMEMADE BONE BROTH

PREPARATION

1. Preheat the oven to 475 degrees.

2. Roast the bones in a pan for 35 minutes, turning them several times, until the meat is tender and deep brown in color. They will finish cooking in the broth.

3. Place all the ingredients and cold filtered water in a large stock pot. Use whatever vegetables you have in your house; they do not need to be finely chopped.

4. Simmer for about an hour and a half, stirring occasionally. The smell should be very aromatic. You can use it now or continue simmering for another 45 minutes.

5. Strain the mixture, pour the broth into containers, and use it in recipes or simply to drink.

NOTE
Bone broth is said to support gut health and is a great drink to start your day, especially if you do not feel your best.

INGREDIENTS

2 pounds beef bones

3 carrots, roughly chopped

3 celery stalks, roughly chopped

1 onion, quartered

½ bunch parsley or basil

1 tablespoon whole black peppercorns

½ cup apple cider vinegar

2 teaspoons ground ginger

cold filtered water to cover the bones, plus 1" above

CHAMOMILE TEA

Makes 1 perfect cup

INGREDIENTS

8 ounces boiling water

loose chamomile tea

quarter of a lemon

2 teaspoons honey

4 thin slices fresh ginger or a half
 teaspoon of powdered ginger,
 optional

PREPARATION

1. We prefer loose chamomile, but tea bags are fine too. If you're using loose tea, place a heaping teaspoonful in a tea steeper and steep until the liquid is dark yellow in color.

2. Remove the steeper and pour the tea into a mug. Squeeze the lemon quarter into the liquid, avoiding the seeds. Add the honey and stir until it dissolves.

3. If you have indigestion or a sore throat, add a half teaspoon of powdered ginger or grate a thumbnail of fresh ginger into the liquid and stir. Allow it to cool or drink it piping hot.

PORK TENDERLOIN *with* BAKED APPLES

PREPARATION

1. Place pork tenderloin in a large ziplock bag, along with the liquid aminos, seasonings, and onion. Refrigerate 4–6 hours or overnight.

2. Preheat the oven to 350 degrees.

3. Transfer the marinated tenderloin to the middle of a baking dish. Spread the sliced apples around the pork and top with the remaining marinade.

4. Roast for 25–30 minutes or until the thickest part of the pork reaches an internal temperature of 140 degrees. Transfer to a plate and let it sit, covered with foil. Prick the apples with a fork to see if they are tender. If they are not, place them back in the oven and allow to cook for an addition 10–15 minutes or until fork-tender.

5. When the apples are tender and the meat has rested, slice the tenderloin ½" to 1" thick, top with the applies and gravy, and garnish with rosemary.

NOTE

To create a gravy for the top, add the remaining liquid in a saucepan. Add ½ cup beef or vegetable stock and scrape up the flavorable bits from the bottom of the baking dish. Add a tablespoon of butter to thicken the mixture and simmer until the sauce has thickened. Pour on top of the meat or serve on the side.

Serves 4–6

INGREDIENTS

1–1½ pound pork tenderloin

2 tablespoons coconut liquid aminos (or soy sauce)

1 teaspoon paprika

salt and pepper to taste

½ teaspoon cinnamon

½ onion, diced

2 big apples, peeled, cored, and sliced

2 rosemary sprigs for garnish

GLUTEN-FREE APPLE CROSTATA

Dough Preparation | Filling | Assembly

Serves 4–6

DOUGH PREPARATION

1. Add the dry ingredients to a food processor and pulse to combine. Repeat with the cold butter and then with the apple cider vinegar and honey or maple syrup. Slowly add the water and pulse until the dough looks flaky. It shouldn't be too dry or too wet to the touch.

2. Place the dough on a floured surface and shape it into a ball. Slice the dough in half and use the other half another time. Place the other half in the refrigerator for 20–30 minutes. Let it rest at room temperature for 15–20 minutes.

ASSEMBLY

1. Preheat the oven to 375 degrees.

2. Prepare the filling by coating the apples with the lemon juice in a bowl. Add the sugar, spices, salt, vanilla or maple syrup, and cornstarch and combine.

3. Sprinkle some flour onto parchment paper and roll the dough into an 8"–10" circle. It shouldn't be too thick, but thick enough to hold the apples in its shell. If the dough cracks, patch it up as you go.

4. Place the parchment paper and dough on a baking sheet. Gently spoon the filling into the middle, spreading it out as you go.

5. Fold the dough's edges to contain the apples, and patch any cracks that appear. Create a pattern with the top layer of apples if you wish.

6. Use an egg wash to lightly coat the edges and place it into the oven. Bake the crostata, rotating it if necessary to ensure even baking. When the crust is golden brown and the apples are soft to the touch—50 to 55 minutes—remove it from the oven and allow it to cool.

INGREDIENTS

Gluten-Free Crust

2½ cups gluten-free flour (try **1½** cups almond flour and **1** cup oat flour)

½ teaspoon salt

2 sticks unsalted, cold European or good Irish butter. To make it dairy-free, use your favorite nondairy butter sticks.

½ teaspoon apple cider vinegar

1 teaspoon honey or maple syrup

½ cup cold filtered water

Filling

3–4 apples, such as Pink Lady, peeled, cored, and thinly sliced

2 tablespoons fresh lemon juice

3 tablespoons white sugar

¼ teaspoon cinnamon, or enough to coat the apples

⅓ teaspoon nutmeg

⅓ teaspoon ginger powder

dash of pumpkin pie seasoning, optional

3 pinches salt

1 capful of vanilla extract or **1** teaspoon maple syrup

1 teaspoon cornstarch or tapioca starch

1999

In late 1999, my mom was expecting her last child—me. This time she was sicker than she had been with my siblings, yet she worked up until the last few days before giving birth.

My parents knew they were having a girl, but they kept it a secret because I was to be the last child and the final girl. Bets were placed at the Ardmore store, balloons were tied to every surface, and the energy around the store was palpable.

On the day I was born, my older siblings were at home with my grandfather, and Philip was with my mom's mom, to whom he was very attached. My other grandmom, Mama Carlino, was in the hospital waiting room, impatiently waiting for me to be born. She tried to fight her way into the birthing room at one point because she could not wait any longer for me to arrive.

My favorite part about my birth story, though, is that my dad was eating a hoagie—yes, a hoagie—while my mom pushed and screamed. He claims, "I hadn't eaten all day, and I was starving and stressed." Honestly, I would be more shocked if he hadn't eaten something.

It seems that I had a flair for the dramatic, even then. Possibly because my mom was working behind the counters, constantly bending to pick up trays and scoop food, the umbilical cord was wrapped tightly around my neck when I was born. I came out purple and not breathing—the baby version of Violet from Willy Wonka. After many rounds of smacking my back and IV infusions, I was screaming and ready to party.

When my grandmom came into the delivery room and saw that I was a girl, she began to cry; she knew how badly my dad had wanted another little girl. I'm told she looked at me like I hung the stars in the sky, as did my grandfather when he first saw me. He always told me I was *la stella del mondo*, and I was never to forget it.

They named me for Nadia Comăneci, the gymnast who dominated the 1976 Olympics, years before I was even a thought, and also for my mom's childhood friend. As a girl

Mama (my grandmother) and me. This picture always brings a smile to my face.

in Italy, she was close to two girls, Nadia and Marina, and has always loved the name Nadia. When I was born, she had her chance to honor the friend she had been separated from since age nine, when her family immigrated to the US. So, there I was: opportunity cinched; gold medal won.

I got my middle name, Elena, from my grandmother's mom, the prayerful sage of the family. Nadia Comăneci's middle name is also Elena, but that is just a coincidence. My great-grandmother Elena was a big part of my family's life. When she was a young child, Elena lived in Brazil due to her father's work placement and the war ravaging Italy. After returning to Italy at age two, courthouse officials changed her name from Elena to Irena.

When my parents had called her with news of the pregnancy, she told them it would be a girl. My parents were dumbfounded; they had not planned on having another child any time soon. However, the women in my family are very intuitive and religious. They always know things before you do, and they will go to great lengths to protect you, even after death. I never got to meet her, but I know in my heart that she is happy I was named in her honor.

When speaking of his grandparents, my dad always told us that they had a love that traveled across the ocean. That love traveled across dimensions and time too.

There are few things I love more than garden salad and lemon bars, although my dad's shrimp and lemon risotto is a close third. My body no longer tolerates dairy, which is an outrage as an Italian. But I still stick primarily to things I knew and loved as a child, and one of those things was fresh garden salad with grilled ciabatta bread. On a hot summer's day, it is the perfect lunch or side dish. It is refreshing, light, and the epitome of summer.

Baby Angela and Nonna Elena (my great-grandmother)

GARDEN TOMATO SALAD *with* GRILLED CIABATTA

PREPARATION

1. In a large mixing bowl, combine the tomatoes, cucumbers, celery, onions, and basil.

2. Add 4–6 ice cubes and stir again.

3. Place the undressed salad in the refrigerator for 1–2 hours before dressing and serving so that it is very chilled. Allowing the assembled salad to sit allows the tomatoes to break down a bit, and the ice melts, so the olive oil added later can create a delicious dressing.

4. Preheat the oven to 400 degrees. Cut off the top of the garlic bulb and place it on a sheet of aluminum foil. Drizzle with olive oil, rubbing it into the cut garlic clove tops. Sprinkle with salt and pepper. Wrap the garlic in the foil and roast for 40–45 minutes.

5. When ready to serve the salad, add the olive oil and salt and pepper. Stir until combined, and add more salt and pepper if needed.

6. Grill the ciabatta slices on a grill top, or toast in a preheated oven for a few minutes. Squeeze the garlic bulb until the garlic paste comes out of the tops, and spread onto the pieces of toasted bread.

7. Arrange the ciabatta on a serving platter. Spoon the tomato salad onto each piece, drizzle some juices over them, and serve.

NOTE

This salad is best in the summer, when tomatoes and cucumbers are at peak season. If you have a tomato and herb garden, this salad will be a summertime meal staple. If you do not have a garden, buy the produce from a farmers' market or grocery market that carries local, seasonal produce.

Serves 3–4

INGREDIENTS

4 medium tomatoes, preferably beefsteak or Roma tomatoes, cut into small wedges

1 seedless English cucumber, thickly sliced in half moons

2 stalks celery, small dice

½ red onion, thinly sliced

1 small bunch fresh basil, roughly chopped

kosher salt and pepper, to taste

ice cubes, for marinating

1 whole garlic bulb

½ cup extra-virgin olive oil

1 loaf Italian ciabatta bread, sliced

RASPBERRY LEMON BUDINO

Serves 4

INGREDIENTS

Lemon Budino

⅓ cup sugar

2 tablespoons water

2½ teaspoons lemon zest

¼ cup lemon juice

⅓ cup whole milk

1 cup heavy cream

2 large egg yolks

pinch of salt

1 tablespoon + ½ teaspoon cornstarch

Lemon Budino

PREPARATION

1. In a small saucepan, combine the sugar, water, lemon zest, and juice. Bring the mixture to a boil and cook until the sugar has dissolved. Remove the saucepan from the heat and let it cool for about 10 minutes.

2. In the same saucepan, slowly whisk in the milk and heavy cream. In a separate bowl, whisk together the egg yolks, salt, and cornstarch until everything is smooth.

3. Slowly add about ¼ of the cream mixture from step 2 to the egg yolks, whisking continuously. Then fold the egg mixture back into the remaining cream.

4. Over medium-low heat, bring the mixture to a boil. Pour it through a fine-mesh strainer to remove any egg that may have cooked.

5. Pour the mixture into four 3–4-ounce ramekins and refrigerate the budino until it is set and chilled, about 2 hours.

6. Top with the raspberry coulis and allow to it set for an additional 30 minutes.

Raspberry Coulis

PREPARATION

1. In a small saucepan, heat the sugar and water over medium heat, stirring until the sugar dissolves completely, about 5 minutes.

2. Transfer the mixture to a blender, add the raspberries and lemon juice, and blend until smooth. Strain the mixture through a fine-mesh sieve to remove the seeds.

3. Add about 1½ teaspoons of the coulis on top of the budino and enjoy as it is, or refrigerate for 30 minutes to an hour to set.

INGREDIENTS

Raspberry Coulis

4 tablespoons sugar

2 tablespoons water

6 ounces fresh or frozen and thawed raspberries

1 teaspoon fresh lemon juice

NOTE
The coulis will last in the refrigerator for 45 days, tightly covered.

When I was in middle school, the school bus dropped me off on a corner near our Ardmore store. I would carry my oversized backpack through the store, trying desperately not to knock things off the counters or eat everything in sight.

Once I put my book bag down, all bets were off. I would always get whatever deli item or cold salad had been on my mind all day, and then I would get a dessert. It was no surprise that I was a chunky kid, but it was worth the pesky comments and the pictures I try not to look at.

Almost every day, I would eat a soufflé cup of raspberry and lemon budino in absolute bliss. I would sit on the tiny chair in the office like a dad after a long workday. I put my legs up and my hands on my distended belly. While this recipe contains dairy, I still cherish it for the memories—and it is too perfect to change.

SHRIMP & LEMON RISOTTO

My dad's risotto remains a comfort food. He is known for his wonderful concoctions, and it was not until Philip and I developed dietary restrictions that he had to get more creative with ingredients for this dish. Following is one of my favorite dairy-free, gluten-free, and garlic-free dishes: his lemon risotto with chickpeas. He includes Parmesan rinds and some loose Parmesan in his recipe to help give it a salty, creamy flavor. Parmesan is technically lactose-free due to its pasteurization process. It is one of the only cheeses my brother and I can tolerate.

Serves 4

INGREDIENTS

Shrimp Stock

shells from **1** pound frozen shrimp

5 cups water, lightly salted with sea salt

½ teaspoon Old Bay seasoning

Shrimp Stock

PREPARATION

1. In a medium saucepan, bring the sea-salted water to a boil and add the shrimp shells. Boil for about 15 minutes or until the liquid begins to reduce.

2. Add the Old Bay seasoning and lower the heat to a slight simmer for another 15 minutes.

3. Reduce the heat to very low to keep the stock hot while continuing to prepare the risotto.

Risotto

PREPARATION

1. In a large skillet, sauté the chopped onion in the olive oil and sea salt until it is golden brown.

2. Add the rice and stir until fully coated in the onion and olive oil mixture. Toast the rice for about 2 minutes, allowing it to become fragrant.

3. Add the white wine and cook until the wine has evaporated and the rice has absorbed almost all the liquid. Be sure to stir often.

4. Add 1 cup of the hot shrimp stock and stir frequently until the liquid is absorbed. Continue by adding hot stock ½ cup at a time, stirring continuously, until the liquid is absorbed.

5. At the 10-minute mark, add the shrimp and continue adding the broth in ½-cup increments for 10 additional minutes, or until the rice reaches al dente.

6. Remove from the heat and add the Parmigiano Reggiano, lemon zest, and lemon juice. Season with salt to taste and top with fresh parsley.

INGREDIENTS

Risotto

1 medium onion, small diced

6 tablespoons olive oil

1 teaspoon sea salt

¾ pound arborio rice

1½ cups white wine

1 pound frozen shrimp, chopped

1 cup Parmigiano Reggiano cheese (optional)

juice and zest of **1** lemon

parsley for garnish, roughly chopped

NOTE
If you do not wish to include Parmesan, the final product will still turn out delicious. Make sure to adjust salt to taste and add some nutritional yeast or dairy-free Parmesan for extra flavor and creaminess!

2000

In August 2000, my family decided to throw my grandfather Nicola a surprise seventieth-birthday party. He was born in late August, but his personality was more of a Leo than a Virgo. He thrived on attention. One of the best ways to show love to him was through public acts; that led to the idea for a surprise birthday party.

According to my dad, the party was one of the best they had ever thrown. Not just because of the beautiful food and setup, but also because it ran according to plan. My grandfather's brother, Amedeo, or George as he loved being called, and his wife, Philomena, took my grandparents to the beach for the weekend, long enough so my parents could prepare.

My grandfather also loved when everything went his way, so getting him to follow the plan was tricky. My parents did not want him to come home until late afternoon. Not one to go with the flow, he insisted on leaving the beach earlier, but his brother managed to stall him until all was prepared.

The guests started arriving at the house before 4 p.m., parking at the nearby St. Raphaela's lot to avoid detection. It worked. When my grandfather walked into the scene and saw everyone there for him, he was genuinely surprised and delighted.

Close to 120 friends, family, and coworkers showed up. A family friend played Italian music on his accordion and sang. Flowers and candles floated in the pool, and tables were set with beautiful white tablecloths. Of course, my grandfather's garden was in full bloom. It was an evening to remember. He often reminisced about that party and how much fun he had with everyone.

As for food, my family stuck with the mantra "simple yet plentiful," so there were many side dishes and a few entrées to choose from. Some of my favorites were Tuscan farfalle with sun-dried tomatoes, pine nuts, and balsamic; chicken saltimbocca; and my grandfather's concoction, mountain-style beans.

My family loved spending time at Uncle Phil's tiny cabin in the mountains. When I say tiny, I mean basically a shack with dormitory beds. My grandfather's recipe for mountain-style beans, or "hearty bean salad," as our stores adapted and named it, originated in that cabin.

Essentially, he took whatever canned beans he had in the cabin; mixed it with some olive oil, salt, and pepper; and called it a day. Over time, we adapted it and made it our own, but it will always remind me of my grandfather and the days after school when he would make this dish and help me devour it with gusto.

This picture was taken at my grandfather Pop's surprise party. He is in the center with Philip on his lap,
Mama behind them, and my siblings on either side.

TUSCAN FARFALLE *with* SUN-DRIED TOMATOES, PINE NUTS *&* BALSAMIC VINEGAR

Serves 4

INGREDIENTS

1 pound farfalle

1 cup pine nuts

½ jar sun-dried tomatoes in oil, chopped

1 cup Parmigiano-Reggiano, shaved

salt and pepper to taste

olive oil and balsamic vinegar, to taste

basil, for garnish

PREPARATION

1. Cook the farfalle pasta in a pot of salted boiling water, and once it is al dente, drain the water. Run cold water over the pasta until it is cool. It can also be refrigerated to make the next day.

2. While the pasta is cooking, toast the pine nuts by adding them to a small saucepan over medium-high heat. Continually stir the pine nuts with a wooden spoon, approximately 3 minutes. Remove from the heat and set aside to cool.

3. In a large bowl, toss together the pasta, sun-dried tomatoes, pine nuts, and Parmigiano-Reggiano cheese. Add salt and pepper to taste, and coat the pasta salad lightly with olive oil and balsamic vinegar. Stir everything together. Garnish with chopped basil, if desired.

CHICKEN SALTIMBOCCA

PREPARATION

1. Place the chicken breasts on a large sheet of parchment paper, season with salt and pepper on both sides, and lightly dredge the chicken in flour.

2. Top each piece of chicken with two sage leaves and one slice of prosciutto. Use a toothpick to secure the sage and prosciutto to the chicken.

3. In a large skillet on high heat, add ¼ cup olive oil and 2 tablespoons of butter. Add the chicken breasts in batches and cook for approximately 3 minutes on each side or until the prosciutto begins to shrink. Transfer the cooked chicken to a dish and repeat until all the chicken is cooked.

4. Wipe out the skillet and return it to the stovetop. Add the remaining 2 tablespoons of butter and the wine and cook until it is reduced by half, 2–4 minutes.

5. Add the stock and bring it to a boil. Continue cooking until it is reduced by half. Return the cooked chicken to the skillet with the prosciutto side up and let it simmer over low heat until the chicken is cooked through, 3–4 minutes.

6. Remove the skewers, then transfer the chicken to a serving platter, pour the stock mixture evenly on top, and serve immediately.

Pictured on page 48

Serves 6

INGREDIENTS

6 thin chicken breasts, skinless and boneless

flour for dredging

salt and pepper, to taste

12 fresh sage leaves

6 thin slices imported prosciutto

¼ cup olive oil

4 tablespoons butter, divided

½ cup white wine

1½ cups chicken stock

MOUNTAIN-STYLE BEAN SALAD

Serves 4–6

INGREDIENTS

½ cup red kidney beans

½ cup cannellini beans

½ cup ceci beans

½ cup black beans

1 red bell pepper, finely chopped

1 yellow bell pepper, finely chopped

1 large carrot, finely chopped

2 large celery stalks, finely chopped

4–5 green onions, finely chopped

½ bunch fresh parsley, finely chopped

1 bunch fresh basil, finely chopped

Salad Dressing

⅓ cup extra-virgin olive oil

4 tablespoons red wine vinegar (or to taste)

salt and pepper to taste

PREPARATION

1. The traditional way of making this recipe is to soak the beans in water for at least 6 hours and then cook for 45 minutes to 2 hours, depending on the beans, using enough water to cover the beans. If you are pressed for time, use canned organic beans.

2. Prepare the dressing by adding the olive oil, vinegar, and salt to a large mixing bowl.

3. If you are cooking the beans from scratch, drain them and add them to the dressing while they are still warm.

4. Add the vegetables and herbs to the bowl, stir until well combined, and let sit for 20–30 minutes, allowing the salad to marinate. Chill the bean mixture after marinating, or serve at room temperature.

2004

Surprise parties are a big thing in our family. In late May 2004, my dad threw my mom a surprise fortieth birthday party at our house with our closest family and friends. My mom's recollection of this story is my favorite rendition, so here it is from her perspective.

My mom recalls the day of the party vividly and in hilarious detail. At the store that day, she was asked to do every little thing. As she put it, "Everyone kept coming up to me asking me to do all the tiny grunt work, and at first, it was fine, but after a while, it was starting to really tick me off."

My grandmother took the day off, saying she didn't feel good. Then my grandfather took off too, supposedly to take care of her. While my dad was in and out of the store getting ready for the party, my mom was left with the menial tasks.

Toward the end of the workday, a manager told my mom that they were getting a big order ready for a very important customer and needed her help. Little did she know that she was essentially helping to prepare the food for her own party.

Later, my dad called my mom and asked her to come home quickly because my grandmother was very sick and needed help feeding the kids. My mom was worried and left as quickly as she could. When she arrived, she was ushered to the back of the house, where everyone was gathered. When they screamed, "Surprise!," she claimed that she "almost had a heart attack."

At first, she was mad that they had lied to her about my grandmother being sick, because she was worried. However, she couldn't hold a grudge long because of how wonderful the day had turned out.

At my mom's surprise party, she held my brother Philip, while my grandfather held me between him and Mama.

As most of our parties went, the accordion player / singer was in full swing, the food was abundant, and the best gift came last. Philip, about nine at the time, wrote my mom a birthday card that still hangs in her closet today. She said it was funny and made her day every time she looked at it.

As for the food, we took our traditional route of delicious yet simple and made some of our staples. The meal included chicken spiedini on the barbecue, Italian-style spareribs, string beans and potatoes, and a strawberry and banana cream shortcake for dessert.

As an anthropology minor, I find the history of culture and food fascinating, so I researched and found that chicken spiedini had originated in my family's hometown region of Abruzzo, Italy. Spiedini is essentially an Italian version of a kebab. However, the name *spiedini* translates to spit (i.e., cooking meat over a fire in a spit).

In the 1900s, an Abruzzese family immigrated to New York and introduced spiedini to the American people. All that to say, we kept the tradition and made this classic for my mother's birthday dinner. Though my family is from Abruzzo, many recipes overlap with other regions as families mingle and share family or regional recipes. Along came the Italian-style spareribs with balsamic glaze, which is prominent in the region of Tuscany.

Last, my family often does string beans and potatoes because it is simple yet flavorful. It utilizes chunks of warm potatoes and soft yet crunchy string beans to create an excellent combination of flavor and texture in one bite. It is the perfect side dish for any entrée.

My family decided on a strawberry banana cream shortcake for dessert because it is a family favorite we gravitate toward regardless of the occasion. The sweetness of the strawberries mixed with the decadent flavor of the cake and the banana cream creates the perfect balance of softness and sweetness with every bite.

CHICKEN SPIEDINI

PREPARATION

1. Cut the chicken into 1" cubes and place in a large bowl. Add rosemary, lemon zest, olive oil, and salt and pepper. Stir until thoroughly combined. You can use the chicken immediately or let it marinate for a few hours in the refrigerator until you are ready to use it.

2. Heat the grill to high. While it is heating, push the chicken onto the wooden skewers and place them on a baking tray.

3. Place the skewers on the grill and reduce the temperature to medium high. Cook for roughly 5 minutes on each side, or until they are browned and cooked thoroughly.

4. Transfer the chicken skewers to a serving plate and add freshly squeezed lemon to taste.

Serves 6–8

INGREDIENTS

4 boneless chicken breasts

3 sprigs fresh rosemary, finely chopped

zest of **1** large lemon

5 tablespoons olive oil

1 tablespoon sea salt

1½ teaspoons freshly ground black pepper

lemon juice for serving

wooden skewers; soaked in a tray of water for 30 minutes

STRING BEANS & POTATOES

Serves 4

PREPARATION

1. In a large saucepan, combine the potatoes and enough salted water to cover the potatoes by 1". Bring to a boil and cook for 10 minutes.

2. Add the beans and cook for about 10 more minutes.

3. Drain the potatoes and string beans. Place the olive oil and garlic in a sauté pan and cook until the garlic is golden.

4. Add the cooked potatoes and beans to the sauté pan and stir. Add salt and pepper to taste.

INGREDIENTS

1 pound potatoes, peeled and large diced

salted water

2½ pounds fresh string beans, trimmed

3 tablespoons extra-virgin olive oil

4–5 garlic cloves, peeled and sliced

freshly ground pepper to taste

ITALIAN-STYLE RIBS *with* BALSAMIC GLAZE

Serves 4–6

INGREDIENTS

2 pounds sparerib racks
    (approximately 2 racks)

3 tablespoons extra-virgin olive oil

1 tablespoon Worcestershire sauce

kosher salt and black pepper,
    to season

3 sprigs fresh rosemary, chopped

red pepper flakes

2 cloves garlic, chopped

¼ cup aged balsamic vinegar,
    divided

½ cup water

2 teaspoons honey

PREPARATION

1. Rinse and pat the spareribs with a paper towel to dry.

2. In a medium mixing bowl, combine the olive oil, Worcestershire sauce, salt, pepper, rosemary, red pepper flakes, garlic, and 2 tablespoons of balsamic vinegar.

3. Season the ribs generously with the rub mixture, making sure to cover both sides of the racks. Cover and refrigerate for approximately 6 hours.

4. When ready to cook, remove the ribs from refrigeration and bring to room temperature (approximately 20 minutes).

5. In a small saucepan over medium heat, combine the remaining balsamic vinegar, water, and honey. Bring to a slight boil, stirring occasionally, until the liquid becomes syrupy, watching carefully so it doesn't burn. Set aside.

6. Grill the spareribs, rib side down, over medium heat for approximately 30 minutes. Then baste the ribs with the balsamic sauce, using a marinating brush.

7. Turn the spareribs to the other side and repeat the basting. Continue to grill for another 30 minutes. Baste periodically until all the glaze is used. To ensure they are fully cooked, pierce the meat with a fork. If it is tender but not falling apart, it is done.

8. Remove from the heat and allow the ribs to cool for about 15 minutes. Cut between the bones and serve.

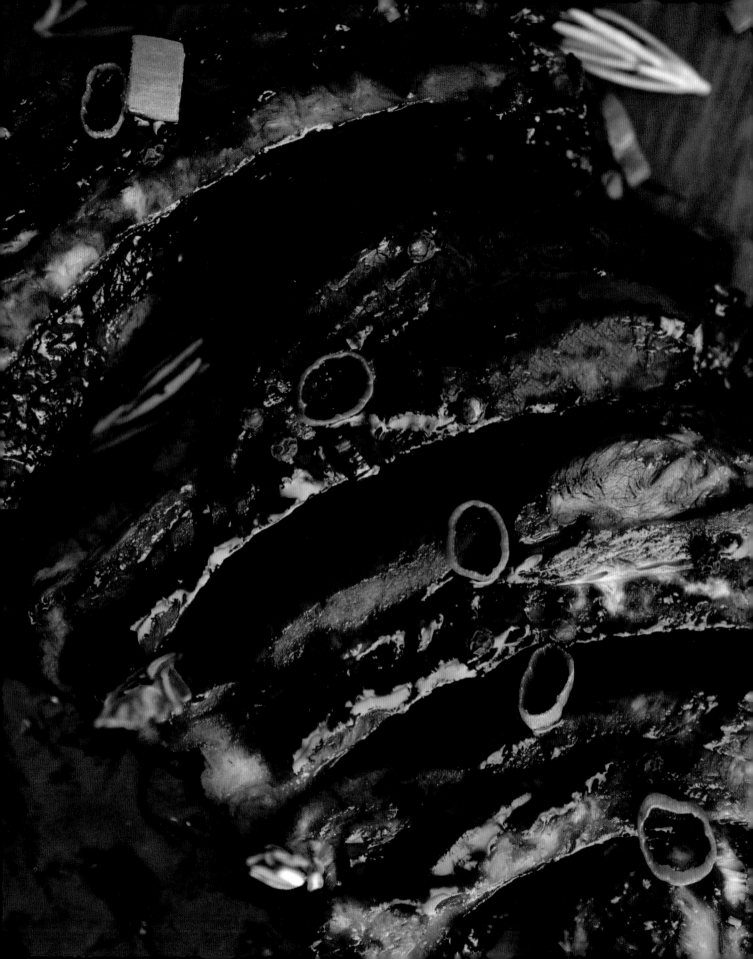

STRAWBERRY BANANA CREAM SHORTCAKE

Serves 8–12

INGREDIENTS

Simple Syrup

2 cups sugar

2 cups water

⅓ of a lemon's juice and peel

⅓ of an orange's juice and peel

cinnamon stick

Strawberry Banana Cream

1 cup strawberries, quartered, extra for decoration

1 tablespoon sugar

1 cup banana, sliced, extra for decoration

1 quart heavy cream

2 tablespoon good-quality vanilla

⅛ cup powdered sugar

PREPARATION

Simple Syrup

In a small saucepan, combine all the ingredients and boil until the sugar is dissolved. Set it aside to cool, and save to use for your recipes.

Strawberry Banana Cream

1. In a small bowl, combine the quartered strawberries and sugar, then set aside.

2. In another small bowl, combine the sliced banana and ¼ cup of the simple syrup; set aside.

3. For the icing, beat the heavy cream, powdered sugar, and vanilla in a mixer until soft peaks form.

4. Combine the strawberries and bananas and drain their syrups into another bowl to use for the cake assembly.

5. Carefully cut the chiffon cake in half (see page 83) and, using a pastry brush, brush both layers with the simple syrup you just made from the drained liquid to moisten the layers.

6. Spread a thin layer of the whipped cream frosting on the bottom layer and add the strawberry-and-banana mixture on top. Place the next layer of cake on top and add the remaining frosting. Decorate with fresh strawberries and bananas.

My mom cutting a strawberry banana cream cake

That's how I loved you in the end. With my body cold and shuddering.
With empty hands over smoldering ash, counting out the minutes.

—LANG LEAV

2005

In 2005, my grandparents Nicola and Angela celebrated their fiftieth wedding anniversary. They met in Italy and eloped when my grandmother was seventeen and my grandfather was twenty-three. Some of their family members disapproved of the marriage, but that didn't stop them. One could say that their love was magnetic—it was truly love at first sight.

It was only fitting that their fiftieth-anniversary celebration be one of extravagance and pure beauty, since their wedding day was not. The event began with everyone accompanying my grandparents to Our Mother of Good Counsel Church, where they renewed their vows.

When they reached the part in the ceremony where the officiant asks the bride if she takes this man to be her husband, my grandmother jokingly said, "I don't know," to which everyone burst out laughing. Later about 250 guests headed to Overbook Country Club for dinner. Some came from as far away as Italy, Canada, and Australia.

I don't remember much from that evening, but I remember the gold outfit my grandmother wore. The top was a silky, silver-gold number with a mesh-like sequined jacket paired with a skirt that perfectly matched the jacket. She looked radiant.

After many speeches, toasts, stories, and dancing, we topped off the evening with an after-party at our house. There were tables of food on the upper level and alongside the pool, and the usual Italian singer and a dance section on the lower level.

My grandparents and dad (*right*) arriving at the church before Mama and Pop's vow renewal. Mama looked radiant.
This is how I picture her waiting for us in the next life.

The sisters from neighboring St. Raphaela's Center also came to celebrate the occasion. The food was nothing less than fabulous, of course. My dad had made his fresh cherry cognac that was perfect for the heat. One of the appetizers was focaccia with garlic, olive oil, and anchovies. The entrées included Italian porchetta paninis with rapini, and fried Italian long hot peppers that were to die for.

What makes a Carlino party an event to behold isn't complicated recipes or setups; it is the simplicity, beauty, and feeling of comfort. Many of the dishes are not particularly difficult to make; rather, the joy of being together makes everything just that much better. That, plus homemade wine and the companionship of family and friends, is what makes an event a party—nothing more, nothing less.

From left to right: Nick, my mom, Philip, Pop, Mama, me, my dad, and Angela before leaving for the vow renewal ceremony

My grandparents with Pop's family, who came from Italy for the occasion. Many of them still live there or have passed on.

My dad making focaccia

62

FOCACCIA *with* GARLIC, OLIVE OIL & ANCHOVIES

PREPARATION

1. Add flour, yeast, salt, and olive oil to a large mixing bowl. Stir using a fork until just combined.

2. Add 2 cups of water and stir until combined. Continue to add water while mixing and gently kneading the dough with your hands until it just comes together into a loose ball.

3. Turn the dough onto a lightly floured surface. Cut the dough ball into halves or quarters to make it easier to knead into smaller dough balls.

4. Knead each dough section by using the heels of your hands, folding the dough in half toward your body and pushing the dough out with the palm of your hand away from your body. Repeat until the dough is soft and still pliable, about 5 minutes.

5. Add about 3 tablespoons of olive oil to a large glass bowl. Use a separate oiled bowl for each dough ball. Roll the dough balls around in the olive oil to lightly coat the entire surface.

6. Cover the bowl in plastic film wrap and a kitchen towel and let it rise until it doubles in size, about an hour. The dough will feel soft to the touch.

7. Transfer the dough ball onto a baking sheet and use your fingertips to dimple the dough, stretching it gently to all sides and corners of the pan. Repeat with each pan of dough.

8. Cover the pans with a kitchen towel and let the dough rise for about 1 hour.

9. Preheat oven to 375 degrees.

10. Using your fingertips, dimple the focaccia. Drizzle olive oil over the surface. Sprinkle the top with sea salt, rosemary, anchovies, and garlic.

11. Bake for 20–25 minutes or until golden brown. Cool to room temperature before serving or using for another recipe.

Makes 2
13" × 9" rectangular loaves or 6
10"–12" round loaves

INGREDIENTS

10 cups all-purpose unbleached flour

4 teaspoons instant yeast

2 teaspoons salt

4–6 tablespoons extra-virgin olive oil, plus **3** tablespoons to oil the bowl

4 cups lukewarm water (72–74 degrees), divided

Topping

extra-virgin olive oil

coarse sea salt

fresh rosemary

6 ounces anchovy fillets in oil

4 garlic cloves, finely chopped

NOTE
If you are storing the bread to use for stuffing, allow the bread to come to room temperature in the pan. Remove it from the pan and cut into ½" cubes. Transfer to a clean baking sheet and let sit uncovered at room temperature for 3–4 days or until dried. Transfer the dried cubes to a freezer-safe gallon bag and freeze until needed.

ITALIAN PORCHETTA PANINI
(ROAST PORK SANDWICHES)

Roast Pork | Au Jus | Rapini (Sautéed Broccoli Rabe) |
Fried Long Hot Peppers

Serves 6–12

INGREDIENTS

6 Italian long rolls, sliced

porchetta (roast pork), prepared

au jus, prepared

broccoli rabe, prepared

fried long hot peppers, prepared

sharp provolone cheese (optional)

Sandwich Assembly

1. Cut the long roll and scoop out a bit of the interior, creating a small depression for the filling.

2. Add the shredded porchetta, au jus, broccoli rabe, and one or two long hot pepper. Top with two slices of sharp provolone.

3. Transfer the open-faced sandwich onto a baking sheet and toast under the broiler 1–2 minutes or until the cheese has melted.

INGREDIENTS

Roast Pork

7-pound boneless pork shoulder

¼ cup extra-virgin olive oil

¼ cup fresh rosemary, chopped

2 tablespoons sage leaves, chopped

1 tablespoon thyme, chopped

6 cloves garlic, minced

zest of 1 lemon

1 teaspoon crushed red pepper
   flakes

3 tablespoon fennel seeds

twine, for tying the roast

1 large onion, peeled and quartered

1 teaspoon coarse black pepper

4 teaspoons kosher saltsalt and
   pepper, to taste

Au Jus

reserved pan drippings from
   porchetta roast

2 cups pork broth (or simply make
   using pork base)

2 sprigs rosemary, chopped

1 tablespoon Worcestershire sauce

salt and pepper, to taste

PREPARATION

Roast Pork

1. Preheat the oven to 450 degrees.

2. Pat the pork dry with paper towels. Set aside while you prep the herb mixture.

3. In a small food processor (or using a mortar and pestle), blend together the olive oil, rosemary, sage, thyme, garlic, lemon, and dried herbs into a paste.

3. Using a sharp knife, score the fat (but not the meat), making ⅛" deep cuts about 1" apart. Rub the pork loin with salt and pepper and place it, fat side up, in a foil-lined roasting pan or rimmed baking sheet.

4. Roll up the roast so that the herbs are nested inside, and tie it with the twine. Add 1 cup of water to the bottom of the pan. Place the pan on the middle rack in the oven.

5. Roast until some of the fat has rendered, 30–45 minutes. Then remove the pan from the oven.

6. Rub the pork with the herb paste mixture (the pork will be hot, so you could use a spoon to rub it on) and carefully place the sliced onion under the pork. Cover it tightly with heavy-duty foil.

7. Place the roast back in the oven and reduce the heat to 325 degrees. Continue to cook for 4–5 hours, until the meat is very tender and the outside is crispy, or until the internal temperature reaches 160 degrees for well done.

8. Transfer the pork to a cutting board or clean roasting pan and let it rest for about 30 minutes.

9. When it is cool enough to handle, use two forks or your fingers to shred the meat. The hard outer skin can be lifted right off and chopped into large pieces. The rest of the meat should be tender enough to pull apart. Adjust the seasoning and arrange on a platter to be served with the rapini and broccoli rabe. Reserve the liquid in the bottom of the pan to prepare the au jus.

PREPARATION

Au Jus

1. Scrape the bottom of the pan to loosen the bits of pork. Carefully transfer the pan juices to a medium saucepan.

2. Add the rosemary and Worcestershire sauce to the pan and cook 4–5 minutes or until the gravy comes to a slow boil. Adjust seasonings and set aside for sandwich assembly.

Rapini (Sautéed Broccoli Rabe)

1. Rinse the broccoli rabe. Trim off the very end of the stems only. Then cut the whole stalk, including the remaining stems, into 2" pieces.

2. Add the broccoli rabe to a large frying pan with ½ cup of water. Cover and cook on high for 5 minutes. Then drain the broccoli and dry with a paper towel.

3. In a clean frying pan, combine the olive oil and garlic and cook for 2 minutes. Add the lemon juice and crushed red pepper and cook for another 2 minutes, being careful not to let the garlic burn.

4. Add the broccoli rabe and cover. Cook for 7–8 minutes or until the stems are soft when pierced with a fork. Set aside for the sandwich assembly.

Pictured on page 60

Fried Long Hot Peppers

1. Preheat oven to 400 degrees.

2. Heat oil in a cast-iron skillet or heavy-bottomed frying pan. Add garlic cloves and peppers and toss in the oil.

3. Transfer the pan to the oven. Bake 10–12 minutes, or until the peppers have blistered. Remove from the pan and set aside for sandwich.

Serves 4–6

INGREDIENTS

Rapini (Sautéed Broccoli Rabe)

1 large bunch rapini (broccoli rabe)

3 tablespoons extra-virgin olive oil

6 garlic cloves, thinly sliced

juice of 1 lemon

crushed red pepper (optional)

salt and pepper, to taste

Serves up to 6

INGREDIENTS

Fried Long Hot Peppers

6 long hot Italian frying peppers

6 cloves garlic, smashed, with skins left attached

¼ cup extra-virgin olive oil

coarse sea salt, to taste

HOMEMADE CHERRY COGNAC

Perfect for an Old-Fashioned

PREPARATION

Cherry Cognac Syrup

1. Take the stems off the cherries and stab them once gently with a fork to ensure they do not split during cooking.

2. Add the water and sugar to a medium saucepan over medium heat and whisk until the sugar dissolves.

3. Add the cherries and vanilla bean and simmer for 3–5 minutes.

4. Strain the cherries and save the liquid in the pan. Place the cherries into a jar (we use tomato sauce jars) and allow the liquid to cool.

5. Once cooled, pour the cognac into the syrup, then pour that mixture over the cherries. Tighten the lid on the jar and allow it to sit in a dark place for at least 6 weeks before making your drinks.

ASSEMBLY

Cherry Cognac Old-Fashioned

1. Rather than using a sugar cube, combine a cherry from the syrup mixture with 3–4 dashes of bitters in a cup. Muddle it with a splash of club soda.

2. Add the bourbon (bourbon brings out the taste of the vanilla in the cognac mixture better than whiskey).

3. Add the ice cube and rub the orange peel around the lip of the glass. Squeeze a bit of the juice from the orange wedge into the glass before placing it in the glass.

4. Add 1 ounce of the cherry cognac syrup to the glass and mix gently until combined. Add some cherries from the syrup mixture to garnish, and enjoy!

INGREDIENTS

Cherry Cognac Syrup

1 pound cherries
(the sweeter the better)

1½ cups sugar

1 cup filtered water

1 vanilla bean, split in half

1 cup cognac
(my dad prefers Remy Martin)

Cherry Cognac Old-Fashioned

1 ounce cherry cognac syrup

3–4 dashes of bitters

splash of club soda

1 ounce bourbon

1 large ice cube

1 orange peel and wedge

That's the thing about love they don't understand. It shapes you in its absence, too.

—AKIF KICHLOO

2007

A few days before her passing, my grandmother had a premonition that she would die. When she died, my world imploded. I was eight years old and cannot remember much of that time, but I do recall that before her massive stroke, there were a few times when she randomly stopped talking and her head dropped, or she would lose consciousness for a few moments. Death was a foreign concept to me, and I thought nothing of it. Now, I realize those incidents were a warning.

In early November 2007, my siblings and I were getting ready for school when we heard our mother screaming. We ran down the stairs to see my dad holding my grandmother's head, trying to talk to her. My mom was on the phone with emergency services, frantically yelling that they needed to hurry. When she saw us, she ordered us back upstairs.

I didn't know what happened. All I knew was that something was wrong with my grandmother, and it wasn't good. I asked my sister, Angela, what happened, and all she told me was that Mama was sick but would be okay. That was all I needed to hear because I trusted her, and so I believed her.

A day or two later, Philip and I visited my grandmother in the hospital after school. She couldn't speak, and she could move only her right side. Even so, as soon as we walked in, her heart monitor started beeping rapidly because she was excited to see us. Despite the fear of hurting her, I ran into her embrace, and I remember wishing she would say something. Anything. Something that would mean she was coming home soon.

When I was in high school, my dad told me that he had wanted to take me to say goodbye before Mama passed, and I responded that I did not need to say goodbye, because she would be okay. He answered that she was not going to make it and would not be coming home. So we went to the hospital. I placed my head on my grandmother's chest and wrapped my body tightly around her like a promise.

On November 4, I vividly remember walking down the hospital's stark white hallway. People were crying, which confused me. I thought they should be happy that they were visiting my grandmother—I was! I didn't know what death was, and I didn't realize it meant goodbye forever.

I remember seeing my grandmother for the last time that day. Her hair was beautifully arranged and her skin

Mama holding me, as she always did

71

still looked warm, but her eyes were closed and she was gone. I didn't shed a tear, because I thought she was sleeping. I trusted her completely and thought she would never leave me.

As my grief-stricken family prepared for the viewing and funeral, I drew countless pictures of all I wished to convey. I placed them on Mama's pillow and asked God to take them to heaven to show her. To my surprise, they were still there when I left the room. My mom placed one of the pictures beside my grandmother in her casket.

The viewing took place over two long, overwhelming days. People I had met before, people I had never met, and people I would never see again were kissing and hugging me. Mama was dressed in her fiftieth-anniversary gown, trinkets were placed next to her, and my picture sat right by her leg, where I used to be when she was alive. This time, her body was cold, and I was coming to understand that she was not going to wake up. That day, I finally shed tears.

Yet, it was not until years later that I fully grieved my grandmother's death. It took until I was fourteen and the death of a close family member for me to process that traumatic experience. As the memories came flooding back, I realized that, in many ways, I was grieving the loss of a mother figure too.

When one part of life ends, another begins. The week my grandmother passed away, we held the grand opening of our new store in West Chester. Despite the beauty of the new store and the countless hours my family spent there, I refused to visit it because I knew it would make my loss real. To this day, it is difficult for me to roam that store. My heart will never be able to disconnect it from the loss of my grandmother. She would have loved it, though.

The recipes in this chapter celebrate our time together. Some of my favorite memories of my grandmother were the days I spent with her after school. We would go upstairs to the office at the Ardmore store and watch the cooking channel.

Another vivid memory was the time my parents went away overnight. My grandmother slept next to me so I wouldn't be alone. As she slept, I remember just staring at her, trying to memorize the curve of her nose, the shape of her face, the sound of her snore, and the way she lightly blew air out of her mouth. I tried to memorize the puff of her hair and the scent of her skin. It felt like her being was meant to be near mine. I feel like she is still at my side, as if she never left.

Earlier in 2007, my other grandmother, Santa DiNardo (my mom's mother), had been rediagnosed with breast cancer after seven years in remission. I found out later that Mom DiNardo had prayed at Mama's funeral, asking God to give her one more year of life. She didn't want us to lose her right after the loss of our other grandmother. Her prayers were answered. It wasn't until November 8, 2008, that she joined Mama in the afterlife. They passed away one year and four days apart.

I don't think we will ever forget Thanksgiving 2007. Losing our first grandmother reminded us to more fully appreciate everything we had. We saw how much we had to lose, and how much we had already lost. We were especially full of gratitude for each other that year.

Despite the overwhelming stress of running the stores during the holidays, we have always hosted a special dinner for family and friends. Thanksgiving 2007 was spent with forty to fifty guests, and we all piled into our kitchen and sunroom for a beautiful meal. In many families, everyone brings their traditional assigned dishes to the feast, and ours is no different. My mom always makes the turkey, with twenty-four hours of prepping. Everyone else brings side dishes and desserts, and homemade wine is brought by anyone who happens to have an open cantina in their basement.

Some Thanksgiving dishes have remained with us through the decades. These include our Italian sausage focaccia stuffing; crispelle; brussels sprouts with dried cranberries, pecans, gorgonzola, maple balsamic, and olive oil; and pumpkin tiramisu for dessert. The recipes have certainly been tweaked and can change from year to year due to allergies or the desire for something new, but these are our classics.

ITALIAN SAUSAGE FOCACCIA STUFFING

PREPARATION

1. Preheat the oven to 350 degrees.

2. Melt 1 tablespoon of the butter with the olive oil in a large skillet over medium-high heat. Add the sausage and break it up into small pieces, using a wooden spoon. Cook thoroughly, 8–10 minutes.

3. Remove the sausage from the skillet and set aside. Drain about half the grease from the pan and add the rest of the butter to the skillet. Sauté the celery and carrots until they begin to soften. Add the onions and cook until they become translucent.

4. In a large mixing bowl, combine the focaccia and the sautéed vegetable mixture. Add the chicken broth. Next, add the beaten egg and stir all the ingredients together.

5. Mix in the sausage and herbs. Add salt and pepper to taste. Transfer the mixture to a greased baking dish and cover with aluminum foil. Bake 40 minutes, then remove the foil and bake until golden, about 15 more minutes.

6. Serve immediately or allow it to cool, and store in the refrigerator until you are ready to use it.

Serves 8–12

INGREDIENTS

3 tablespoons unsalted butter, divided

2 tablespoons extra-virgin olive oil

2 pounds ground Italian sausage, mild, casings removed

2 cups onion, small dice

1 cup celery, small dice

1 cup carrots, small dice

6 cups focaccia cubes, dried (use recipe from page 63)

2 cups chicken broth

2 eggs, beaten

2 teaspoon fresh sage, finely chopped

1 tablespoon fresh parsley, finely chopped

3 tablespoon fresh thyme, finely chopped

freshly ground sea salt, to taste

freshly ground black pepper, to taste

DAIRY-FREE CORN BREAD

Serves 4–6

INGREDIENTS

1 cup cornmeal

1 cup all-purpose flour

⅔ cup white sugar

1 tablespoon baking powder

½ teaspoon salt

1 cup dairy-free milk or water

2 eggs, beaten

⅓ cup extra-virgin olive oil

PREPARATION

1. Preheat the oven to 400.

2. Whisk together the dry ingredients in a medium bowl.

3. Add the wet ingredients and mix until everything is well combined.

4. Pour the mixture into a medium baking pan lined with parchment or coated with nonstick cooking spray. Bake 15 to 20 minutes or until the center is no longer wet. Allow to cool and settle before serving.

ROASTED BRUSSELS SPROUTS *with* GORGONZOLA, CRANBERRIES, PECANS & MAPLE BALSAMIC

PREPARATION

1. Preheat the oven to 350 degrees.

2. Line a baking sheet with aluminum foil or parchment paper and add the pecans. Bake them until they are lightly toasted, about 5 minutes. Be careful, because they burn quickly.

3. Transfer the pecans to a cutting board and chop coarsely. Set aside in a small bowl.

4. Raise the oven temperature to 425 degrees and line the baking sheet with fresh aluminum foil or parchment paper. In a large bowl, toss the brussels sprouts with olive oil, salt, and pepper and place them on the baking sheet.

5. Roast the brussels sprouts for about 20 minutes, stirring halfway through, to ensure they brown and are tender.

6. Once they have cooled a bit, transfer the brussels sprouts to a large bowl. Add the maple syrup and cranberries and toss to coat. Taste the mixture and correct the seasonings if needed.

7. Transfer the brussels sprouts to a serving dish and add the chopped, toasted pecans and gorgonzola. Serve immediately.

Pictured on page 70

Serves 4–6

INGREDIENTS

2 pounds brussels sprouts, halved (stem and ragged outer leaves removed)

½ cup pecans

3½ tablespoons extra-virgin olive oil

1 teaspoon sea salt or kosher salt, or to taste

1 teaspoon freshly ground black pepper, or to taste

3 tablespoons maple syrup

½ cup crumbled gorgonzola

½ cup dried cranberries or craisins

SPICED PUMPKIN TIRAMISU

Serves 6–8

INGREDIENTS

Syrup

1 cup water

1 cup brewed espresso

⅔ cup sugar

⅔ cup hazelnut liqueur

Pumpkin Mixture

1 cup sugar

4 eggs

1½ teaspoons cinnamon

½ teaspoon ground nutmeg

¼ teaspoon ground ginger

¼ teaspoon ground allspice

¾ cup pumpkin puree

1 pound mascarpone

ASSEMBLY

54 crisp ladyfinger cookies

1 tablespoon sugar

½ teaspoon ground cinnamon

PREPARATION

Syrup

1. In a small saucepan, combine all the ingredients and stir constantly over medium-low heat until the sugar has dissolved, about 3 minutes.

2. Transfer the liquid to a shallow bowl to allow it to cool completely.

NOTE
This mixture should be made ahead of time and stored in the refrigerator.

Pumpkin Mixture

1. Over a double boiler, whisk together the sugar and eggs until the mixture is light and creamy, whisking continuously. Cool the bowl over an ice bath.

2. Mix the spices with the pumpkin puree, then slowly mix in the mascarpone.

3. Gently fold the cooled egg mixture into the pumpkin puree.

ASSEMBLY

1. To assemble the tiramisu, quickly dip 18 ladyfingers into the coffee mixture, allowing the excess to drip off. Be sure not to soak them too long, or they will fall apart.

2. Arrange them in a single layer in a 13" × 9" dish. Then spread a third of the pumpkin mixture on top. Repeat steps 1 and 2 for two more layers.

3. Combine the sugar and cinnamon and sprinkle the mixture on top. Cover the tiramisu and refrigerate it to allow it to settle and set for at least 8 hours or overnight.

After everyone filled their plates, we sat down and everyone took turns saying what we were thankful for that year. It was a wonderful tradition that reminded us why we do what we do and what gets us up every morning. That year, our gratitude was mainly filled with tears and wishes that my grandmother was there to share it with us.

In a way, she was. As we enjoyed our meal that late afternoon, Louie, our main chef in West Chester and a close family friend, noticed something outside. Although the weather was very cold and the rose bushes were bare, directly in view of the Thanksgiving table a singular pink rose was blooming. For us, it was a sign of hope. That year, we were grateful for things both seen and unseen.

OPTIONAL

for garnish, add shaved white or dark chocolate and add cocoa powder or cinnamon on top, with cinnamon sticks or anise for a pop of color.

I found this singular pink rose while dividing the flowers for my grandparents' graves. It was Mama's birthday.

8

2010

The year 2010 was a big one for the Carlino family: the oldest child, Angela, was getting married. The wedding preparations were nothing short of a triathlon, but that made it all the more memorable. I had turned eleven about a month before the wedding, so this was a massive event for me. I had experienced more loss and more funerals than weddings in my short life, so this was a big deal.

Traditional Italian wedding ceremonies have multiple components leading up to the main event. This meant that two days before the wedding, my sister's fiancé, Joe, was going to serenade my sister at her window in her childhood home. Our family from Italy came to celebrate, including Uncle Vincenzo, who played the mandolin. At the same time, Joe sang like a dying alley cat at Angela's window.

The serenade tradition is meant to show a suitor's intentions for his love interest. Typically, he will show up at her house and play the accordion—or be accompanied with music—and sing. If he plays two songs, the intention is friendship. If he plays three to four songs, the girl knows he has honorable intentions for a serious courtship leading to a proposal, and he will go inside and celebrate with her family. If the man plays six songs, he loves her.

Another tradition we celebrated that evening was the cooking of the Abruzzese arrosticini, or lamb kebobs. This delicacy was not an easy task to find and prepare, but my dad and his Uncle Frank (Mama's brother) were clearly up to the task. That night, with help from a few other family members, they cooked about three hundred arrosticinis, which were devoured in ravenous fashion. The celebration was nowhere near over, though. At about 3 a.m., another batch of food was prepared, including aglio é olio. This traditional pasta dish certainly helped soak up copious amounts of alcoholic beverages.

ARROSTICINI (LAMB SKEWERS)

Serves 8–10

INGREDIENTS

2 pounds lamb shoulder, rinsed
and patted dry

2 tablespoons extra-virgin olive oil

sea salt and black pepper,
to taste

soaked wooden skewers
(see spiedini recipe on page 55)

PREPARATION

1. Cut the lamb shoulder into small cubes about ⅓" thick. Place the cubes of meat on the skewers, ensuring they are close together and compact.

2. An arrosticini grill is normally used for this, but a regular grill will work too, if it has a grooved skewer section that enables them to cook evenly.

3. When the charcoal turns white, place the skewers on the grilling grooves. Keep turning the skewers to ensure even cooking, and rotate their position on the grill. Add salt while they are cooking. Once the meat is a golden brown and slightly charred, take them off the grill and serve immediately. Add more salt, if necessary.

CARLINO'S AGLIO É OLIO

PREPARATION

1. Add the oil and garlic to a medium saucepan and simmer. When the garlic begins to turn golden, remove it from the heat.

2. Add the anchovies and stir. Add the sun-dried tomatoes to the mixture.

3. Bring the salted water to a boil and add the linguini. When the pasta is al dente, 7–9 minutes, add the pasta to the skillet with the oil and anchovies. Add about a ladleful of the pasta water to the oil mixture and stir until the pasta absorbs the liquid.

4. Add the Parmesan cheese to the pasta and stir until the mixture is fully blended and creamy.

5. Plate the pasta and add freshly chopped parsley to garnish. Add black pepper or red pepper flakes for a small kick.

INGREDIENTS

⅓ cup olive oil

2 garlic cloves, thinly sliced

⅓ can anchovies, chopped (optional)

½ cup sun-dried tomatoes, chopped

4 cups salted water

1 pound linguini

salt, pepper, and red pepper flakes, to taste

fresh parsley and Parmesan cheese for garnish

If there was one thing my grandmother loved, it was a wedding. She had been preparing for Angela's wedding long before Angela had a serious boyfriend. My grandmother never got the wedding of her dreams, and she wanted to ensure that my sister did.

When my grandmother came from Italy, she brought her hope chest. Painted blue and gold, it held handmade linens and tablecloths given to her by my great-grandmother Elena. The hope chest sat beside my grandmother's rocking chair in her room, and she constantly reminded my sister of how important it was. We wouldn't understand how important it was until later.

My grandmother also loved fashion and had said she would buy Angela a wedding dress like Princess Diana's. Although, sadly, she didn't make it to my sister's wedding or help her choose a dress, my grandmother worked in mysterious ways. The day Angela went to try on dresses, she fell instantly in love with a dress that had a sweetheart neckline and beautiful beading on the bodice and waist. It was perfect, and apparently my grandmother thought so too. The woman assisting my sister looked at her in the mirror and said, "You look just like Princess Diana." That was all we needed to hear; that was the dress.

In search of "something old" for the bride to wear, my mom and sister looked through the hope chest, which was filled to the brim. Under the top few items they found a folded envelope wedged between tissue paper layers. In that envelope was cash gathered over an extended period and carefully stowed away. Our grandmother had left a note, half of it written in Italian and half in English, explaining that she wanted Angela to use the money for a dress. She had kept her promise.

On the big day, as everyone was getting ready in Angela's childhood bedroom, a minor calamity occurred. We could not find my bridesmaid's dress! It was genuinely nowhere to be found, and everyone was running around like chickens while trying not to stress out my sister.

After hours of fruitless searching, my mom called her friend Judy, who owns St. Jude's Shop in Havertown, a shop for Catholic supplies. Judy came as fast as lightning with an armful of communion dresses for me to try on.

I was a pretty hefty eleven-year-old, so finding a dress that fit was a challenge. Thankfully, one of the dresses finally zippered, even though I could barely breathe out of one lung, and we were off to the church.

The ceremony was beautiful, the reception was exceptional, and who could forget the extended after-party? There was enough food to feed the masses, along with a phenomenal seven-tiered wedding cake in multiple flavors. It was indeed a night to remember. After an hour of dancing to seemingly every Italian song in existence, I fell soundly asleep on a sofa. It was the perfect end to a wonderful day.

In hindsight, always look where you least expect a lost item to be, or ask the person you least expect to know. A couple of weeks later, my grandfather appeared in the kitchen with my bridesmaid's dress and asked my mom whose dress it was. It turns out that my dress was behind his suit in his room. Despite the commotion around him, my grandfather had been unaware of our crisis. Ignorance truly is bliss, I suppose.

Angela trying to remain calm in her wedding dress despite my bridesmaid dress being MIA.
Here I am, passed out on a sofa at the wedding after-party, while the accordion music blasted.

ANGELA'S WEDDING CAKE

Blackberry Preserves | *Chiffon Cake* | *Italian Meringue Buttercream*

PREPARATION

Blackberry Preserves

1. Place the blackberries in a saucepan and simmer over low heat, stirring continuously until they soften and start to release their juices. With a fork, mash the berries to further release the juice. Remove the pan from the heat.

2. Press the mixture in small spoonfuls through a fine-mesh sieve to strain the seeds. You should have about ¾ cup of juice.

3. Mix 2–2½ tablespoons of the juice in with the cornstarch. Transfer the rest of the juice to a pan and add the honey. Stir in the cornstarch and juice mixture slowly over medium-high heat until it thickens, 3–4 minutes.

4. Remove from the heat and let it cool before placing it into a jar or a bowl in the refrigerator.

INGREDIENTS

Blackberry Preserves

12 ounces blackberries (fresh or frozen)

2 tablespoons honey

1 tablespoon cornstarch

Angela and Joe cutting their seven-tier wedding cake

Serves 8-12

INGREDIENTS

Chiffon Cake

5 cups sugar

5 cups **00** flour

2½ cups water

1 cup canola oil

12 large eggs

1 vanilla bean

1 orange, zested

2 teaspoons baking powder

1 tablespoon plus **1** teaspoon
    cream of tartar

1 teaspoon salt

NOTE

*Angela's cake had seven layers and
served over three hundred people. This
recipe does not need to be tiered and is
perfect for any occasion.*

PREPARATION

Chiffon Cake

1. Preheat the oven to 325 degrees.

2. Sift the flour into a bowl with the baking powder. Add the sugar and salt and combine it all together with a spoon or fork until thoroughly mixed.

3. In a separate bowl, separate the egg yolks, reserving the whites in another small bowl. Add the room-temperature water and oil to the yolks.

4. To the egg yolk mixture, add the lemon zest and the seeds from the vanilla bean. Whisk until it becomes creamy.

5. Add the dry ingredients and continue to whisk until the mixture is smooth and creamy. Set aside.

6. Pour the egg whites into a stand mixer and beat them until frothy, then add the cream of tartar and continue to mix until combined.

7. Add some of the egg yolk mixture to the egg whites and stir briskly. Then add in the remaining egg yolk mixture a small amount at a time and mix gently with a spatula from top to bottom to keep the egg whites fluffy and airy.

8. Pour the mixture gently into a chiffon cake pan (this specialty pan can be found online or in stores). The pan does not need to be coated with butter and flour.

9. Distribute the cake mix evenly and bake on the middle rack for about an hour. Do not put it on the highest rack in the oven, so that it doesn't burn.

10. When it is golden brown in color, remove the pan from the oven. Flip the pan upside down gently to rest it. Allow the cake to cool completely before carefully removing the top of the pan with a knife.

NOTE

Chiffon cake can be eaten with powdered sugar on top, and it is popular in Italy paired with a cappuccino or espresso. Without filling, this cake can be stored 2–3 days in a glass dome or for 3–4 days wrapped tightly and refrigerated.

PREPARATION

Italian Meringue Buttercream

1. Using a stand mixer or hand mixer, beat the egg whites, cream of tartar, and salt. Slowly add half the sugar and continue beating until soft peaks form.

2. Meanwhile, add the remaining sugar and the water to a saucepan on medium-low heat. Stir the mixture until the sugar dissolves. Raise the temperature to medium high and continue cooking until the internal temperature reaches approximately 240 degrees.

3. Add the cooked sugar syrup to the mixer. Soft peaks should have formed by now. Keep mixing until the meringue is cool to the touch.

4. For a stand mixer, use the paddle attachment and slowly add the butter. Then add the salt and vanilla extract, if desired. Keep paddling until the butter is thoroughly combined and the buttercream has reached a beautiful, smooth consistency.

ASSEMBLY

1. Carefully cut the chiffon cake in half. Using a pastry brush, brush the layers with simple syrup (see recipe on page 58) to ensure the layers are moist.

2. Spread the bottom layer of the cake with a thin layer of the lemon meringue buttercream, then top with a thin layer of blackberry preserves. Frost the cake with the remaining Italian meringue buttercream and decorate it to taste.

Serves 10–12

INGREDIENTS

Italian Meringue Buttercream

4 large egg whites

⅓ teaspoon salt

1⅓ cups sugar, divided

1 teaspoon vanilla extract (optional)

15 ounces unsalted butter, at room temperature

¼ teaspoon cream of tartar

⅓ cup filtered water, at room temperature

NOTE

It is best to use the frosting immediately, but if you are storing it, be sure to whip it again to bring it back to life. If it doesn't regain its silky-smooth consistency, place it in the refrigerator for a few minutes until it thickens. Bring it to room temperature and whip it again.

2011

My brother Nick was the first member of my family to graduate with a bachelor's degree. My sister earned an associate degree from St. Joseph's University before pursuing culinary school and becoming Chef Angela.

Nick's accomplishment was not some small feat. He managed to work full-time while attending college and maintaining good grades. He also lost both of our grandmothers during this period. He and my grandmothers were very close, and their loss took a physical and emotional toll on him. He graduated from St. Joseph's University in 2011 with dual degrees in food marketing and Italian, which has helped him push the stores to new heights.

So, if anyone deserved a graduation party, it was Nick. The party took place in our backyard, as most of them did. There was music blaring on speakers, barbecues and stoves on full heat, and cold drinks being poured because of the heat. There were tables filled with antipasti, and my dad was barbecuing anything that was not tied down.

My parents made a caprese pasta salad appetizer and grilled salmon with caramelized onion and feta as one of the main entrées. Our pastry chef Jessica, who has been with us for a long time and trained under Mama, made Italian cream puffs as part of the large spread of desserts. Those cream puffs continue to be one of our classics that are beloved among customers and family alike.

The party was lively until the wee hours of the night. Nick and his friends spent their time in and out of the pool and sipping cocktails. The mixture of the heat, the soft haze of the twinkling lights, and the sound of the reverberating bass and splashing water created an atmosphere that felt profoundly homey. The only thing missing was my grandmothers' presence, but their spirits will always be around.

My parents and Nicky at his graduation ceremony. His chords were from the Italian Honor Society.
Angela and Nick after Nick's graduation ceremony

CAPRESE PASTA SALAD

Serves 4

• ✽ •

INGREDIENTS

½ cup extra-virgin olive oil

½ yellow onion, sliced

1 small green zucchini or yellow
squash, skin on and sliced thick

¾ pound mezze rigatoni

8 ounces fresh mini mozzarella
cheese balls

8 ounces cherry tomatoes

½ cup sliced almonds, lightly
toasted

salt and pepper to taste

balsamic vinegar for light glaze

5 leaves fresh basil, roughly
chopped

PREPARATION

1. Sauté the onion in the oil in a medium saucepan on low heat, until it
softens.

2. Add the sliced zucchini and cook it for 1–2 minutes, stirring constantly.

3. Cook the pasta to package instructions for al dente. Add it to the vegetables
in the saucepan and stir constantly until it is fully coated in oil.

5. Take mixture off the heat and place into a mixing bowl to cool. Then
add the mozzarella, cherry tomatoes, salt and pepper, and lightly toasted
almonds.

6. Add a splash of balsamic vinegar to the bowl and mix. Top with fresh
basil and serve.

Pictured on page 86

GRILLED SALMON *with* CARAMELIZED ONION & FETA

PREPARATION

1. In a mixing bowl, combine all ingredients except the salmon, onions, feta, and olive oil. Stir in 2 tablespoons of olive oil to make a paste. Spread the paste on the salmon fillets and marinate for 30 minutes.

2. In a sauté pan, over medium heat, place the remaining 2 tablespoons of olive oil and sliced onions. Cook until very soft and golden brown.

3. Liberally spray nonstick cooking spray onto a grill heated to 450–500 degrees. Place the salmon skin down and do not flip. Cook for 6–10 minutes or until the thickest portion reaches 120 degrees.

4. Remove the fish from the grill and allow it to rest and finish cooking.

5. Top the fillets with the warm cooked onions and crumbled feta. Serve warm.

Serves 4

INGREDIENTS

4 6-ounce wild salmon fillets

2 large, sweet onions, thinly sliced

1 pound crumbled feta

4 tablespoons olive oil

2 teaspoons black pepper

2 teaspoons paprika

2 teaspoons minced garlic

1 teaspoon cayenne pepper

4 tablespoons Dijon mustard

4 tablespoons brown sugar

ITALIAN CREAM PUFFS

Serves 10

• • •

INGREDIENTS

6 tablespoons all-purpose or **00** flour

6 tablespoons water or milk

2½ tablespoons unsalted butter

1 large egg at room temperature

pinch of salt

NOTE

They can be refrigerated for 1–2 days in an airtight container before they become soggy. They are best eaten the same day or the next morning for breakfast!

PREPARATION

1. Preheat the oven to 430 degrees. Line two baking sheets with parchment paper.

2. Sift the flour into a bowl and set aside.

3. Combine water (or milk), salt, and butter in a medium saucepan, and heat on low until the butter has melted. Then raise the heat to medium and bring the mixture to a boil.

4. Add the sifted flour to the saucepan and stir constantly until the mixture stops sticking to the sides. Remove it from the heat and scrape the mixture into an electric mixer. Allow it to cool for 2 minutes.

5. Beat the mixture for 2 minutes, then add the eggs, one at a time. Mix until the egg has been completely incorporated before adding the next egg. The mixture should be smooth and thick.

6. Drop large teaspoonfuls of the mixture onto a lined baking sheet, using another clean spoon to push the mixture off the spoon.

7. Bake the puffs for about 10 minutes, then turn the oven down to 350 degrees and bake for another 40 minutes. When cooked, cool the puffs in the oven with the door open.

ASSEMBLY

1. When the cream puffs are completely cooled, use the back of a wooden spoon or dowel to make a small hole in the bottom of the cream puff. Spoon the patisserie cream (recipe follows) into a pastry bag and fill each cream puff fully.

2. Allow them to set in the refrigerator for at least 30 minutes or until cooled. Top with powdered sugar and enjoy!

CREMA PASTICCERIA

PREPARATION

1. In a medium electric mixing bowl or with an electric mixer, mix the egg yolks and sugar for about 5 minutes or until foamy. Add the cornstarch and mix it until smooth, about 2 minutes.

2. In a medium saucepan, heat the milk on low heat and add the vanilla bean pod and lemon zest. Stir until fully combined.

3. Turn the heat up to medium and allow it to come to a light boil or until little bubbles start to form on the side. When the milk is warm but not too hot, remove it from the heat and add the egg mixture from step 1, a little at a time, stirring constantly, until everything is fully incorporated.

4. Put the saucepan back onto low heat or simmer and keep whisking for about 4 minutes or until the cream starts to thicken. Make sure the cream doesn't boil, to avoid curdling the eggs. As soon as bubbles start to form, lower the heat. Continue cooking until the cream is thickened, or until it coats the back of a spoon without dripping off.

5. Remove it from the stove and put it into a cold glass jar or bowl. Cover tightly with plastic wrap and refrigerate for at least 3 hours to set.

Serves 10

INGREDIENTS

3 large egg yolks

3½ tablespoons sugar

2½ tablespoons cornstarch

1½ + 2 tablespoons whole milk

1 vanilla pod

zest of half a lemon

2013-2017

One of our family's greatest joys has been the birth of Angela's children. In 2013, I had just started my freshman year of high school when she sat us down and broke the news that she was expecting her first child. At first I was shocked, and then I felt tears of joy.

Angela and I have a significant age gap between us, and when she became pregnant, I felt closer to her. She invited me over often to bake, and we ate as many sweets, cheeseburgers, and pickles as we could in one sitting without getting sick. Those are some of my most cherished memories.

When Vincent was born, it was like the sun was finally shining after a long period of darkness. As a toddler, Vincent never failed to surprise us with his intelligent, curious mind. He also made us feel loved with afternoon cuddles. His timing was perfect, and he was everything we could have asked for.

Two years later, Angela gave birth to Michael. He is quite different from Vincent; Michael's personality is to act now, think later, while Vince is more likely to think everything through before deciding if it is worth pursuing. Together, they are the perfect pair.

When Ang and her husband, Joe, asked Nick and me to be Michael's godparents, I started crying. It was an incredible honor, and one I do not take lightly.

In 2019, I was ready to return to college for the second semester of my sophomore year when our family was once again gathered around the dinner table. My mom's announcement, "I'm pregnant," was met with both laughter and instant repulsion. Then Ang quipped, "She's not pregnant, but I am."

It was difficult being away from my family for most of Ang's pregnancy and the birth, but they made me feel loved, whether it was a daily phone call or a care package of goodies. I was sitting in the campus Starbucks when I got a text message saying that Olivia Marie was born. My sister finally had a girl. I had to get up and pace around campus because my heart felt like it was going to explode.

Angela pregnant with my nephew Vincent. This is one of my favorite pictures of her.

Olivia was beautiful, and still is. She is the piece that we did not know was missing until she was born.

My nephews and niece are the heart of the family. They enrich our lives with their quick humor, infectious laughter, and endless love and hugs. No matter what kind of day we are having, it instantly becomes brighter when we see or FaceTime them. Likewise, when my mom is angry or upset, all I have to do is shove a photo of the kids in front of her face, and she starts to breathe normally again. I just wish my grandmothers were here to see them. They would be in love, and so proud.

Ang had different food cravings during each of her three pregnancies—some that were repulsive, and others that I helped her indulge in. For that reason, I am sharing three recipes. When she was expecting Vincent, she ate pickles straight from the jar and many cheeseburgers. Thus, our famous cheeseburger was born, and it is one of Vincent's favorite meals. There were many nights when I would receive a text from Ang saying, "Want a burger? Don't tell Mom."

During her pregnancy with Michael and Olivia, she was craving more dessert foods, including jelly donuts, sweet fried dough, and creme brûlée. Also, root beer. She drank root beer so often that I gave her a bottle for Christmas with a little bow. Though traditional bomboloni is made with Italian cream, I am substituting it for raspberry filling in memory of Ang's jelly doughnut craving.

Similarly, our recipe for sweet fried dough brings to mind images of my grandmother, Mama, frying it on the stove, a smile on her face. I can only imagine how much Mama would have enjoyed making it for her great-grandchildren.

BOMBOLONI *with* JELLY FILLING

PREPARATION

Filling: See Raspberry Coulis Recipe

1. To make the dough by using a stand mixer or mixing bowl, mix the flour, sugar, and yeast together. Add the cubes of butter, spacing them out in the bowl. Then add the eggs, milk, vanilla extract, and salt. Using a dough hook, mix on low speed until all the ingredients are combined, 8–10 minutes.

2. Using a large, clean surface, knead the dough into a smooth ball. Place the dough in a lightly greased bowl and cover with plastic wrap or a towel. Allow it to proof for 2½–3 hours or until it has tripled in size.

3. Once it has risen, transfer the dough to a clean surface and punch the air out of it lightly before kneading it into another smooth ball. With your hands, flatten the dough and roll it out to make a rectangular shape about ½" thick.

4. Use a glass or a precision cookie cutter to cut out the doughnuts. Don't be afraid to use the leftover dough to make fried dough in all shapes and sizes!

5. Place the cutout doughnuts on parchment paper and cover them loosely with a towel or plastic wrap. Allow the doughnuts to proof for 1–1½ hours, or until they've doubled in size.

6. Fill a large, deep pot about halfway with oil and heat the oil to 337 degrees. Carefully place 3–4 doughnuts at a time into the oil. You may use the parchment paper to slide the doughnuts into the oil, and remove the parchment once the doughnuts are cooking.

7. Fry the doughnuts on each side for about 2 minutes, or until golden brown. Drain them on paper towels and then roll them in sugar. Allow the doughnuts to cool before filling.

ASSEMBLY

1. Using a knife, make a small hole on the side of the doughnut for the pastry bag tip to fit into. Scoop the raspberry coulis into a pastry bag with a standard-size pastry tip, and pipe into the bomboloni until the filling is almost coming out.

2. Dust with powdered sugar, if desired, and serve with coulis on the side.

Makes 10–12 doughnuts

INGREDIENTS

2 cups bread flour

2 cups **00** flour or all-purpose flour

½ cup sugar

2½ tablespoons sugar, for rolling

2¼ teaspoons yeast

pinch of salt

3 eggs, room temperature

6½ tablespoons butter, softened and cubed

½ cup lukewarm **2%** milk

½ teaspoon vanilla extract

canola or vegetable oil for frying

NOTE

If you don't have a pastry bag, snip a corner of a zippered bag, cutting an opening big enough to fill the bomboloni hole. Add the filling, close the bag, and pipe the filling into the doughnut, as you would with a pastry bag.

CARLINO'S *Famous* CHEESEBURGER

Serves 6

INGREDIENTS

pancetta jam, prepared, recipe
follows

1 pound ground beef (80/20
preferable)

1 pound ground pork

6 slices Asiago cheese or **4** ounces
shredded Asiago

salt

black pepper

4 Italian round rolls or brioche buns

4 leaves bib lettuce or baby arugula

onions, preferably Vidalia, thinly
sliced, raw, sautéed, or grilled

Pancetta Jam
Yields approximately 3 cups

INGREDIENTS

10 ounces pancetta, diced (or
thick-cut bacon)

6 large shallots, peeled and sliced
thinly

1 teaspoon olive oil

2 cloves garlic, crushed

½ cup light-brown sugar

3 tablespoons aged balsamic
vinegar

6 tablespoons espresso

1 teaspoon ground black pepper

PREPARATION

Pancetta Jam

1. Place pancetta in a large, high-walled pan over medium heat. Cook until the fat is rendered.

2. Remove the pancetta with a slotted spoon and transfer to a paper-towel-lined plate. Discard the excess fat but don't wipe the pan clean.

3. Return the pan to the stove and cook the shallots over low heat, stirring, 10–15 minutes, until they are caramelized. Transfer the shallots to a bowl.

4. Return the pan to medium heat, add the olive oil and garlic, and sauté for about 1 minute. Add the cooked pancetta, shallots, and the rest of the ingredients to the pan.

5. Turn up the heat and bring the mixture to a boil, stirring continuously for about 2 minutes. Lower the heat and simmer until the liquid is the consistency of thick syrup, 20–25 minutes.

6. Allow the mixture to cool for approximately 20 minutes. Transfer the mixture to a food processor and blend until it reaches a coarse consistency.

7. Store in a jelly jar with a tight seal for up to one month.

ASSEMBLY

1. Place the ground beef, pork, and salt and pepper in a medium mixing bowl. Using your hands, mix the ingredients together until they are just combined. Be sure not to overmix, which will make the meat tough.

2. Separate the burger mixture into 6 equal portions. Place a beef patty between two layers of parchment paper and press down to a ¼" flat patty, using a heavy-bottomed or cast-iron pan or a burger press.

3. Fold a slice of Asiago cheese in half twice to form a small square, or about a tablespoon of shredded Asiago, and place in the center of the beef patty. Then add 1 tablespoon of pancetta jam on top. Close with

another flattened patty by pinching the edges to seal in the cheese and jam. Season the top with freshly ground black pepper and kosher salt.

4. Place the burgers on a hot grill and close the lid. Cook 3–4 minutes per side, or until desired doneness is achieved. Melt another piece of cheese on top, if you like.

5. Assemble each burger on a freshly grilled bun, top with lettuce and onions, and enjoy!

Pictured on page 92

SWEET FRIED DOUGH

PREPARATION

1. Pour the oil into a deep skillet and heat it until it reaches 350 degrees.

2. Slice each pizza dough into 2 even sections and shape and stretch into a disk about 8" in diameter.

3. Place the disks, one at a time, into the oil and cook until golden brown, about 1 minute on each side. Remove and drain them on a plate lined with paper towels.

Quickly add the sugar to both sides and eat when hot.

Serves 4

INGREDIENTS

2 fresh pizza doughs (can be bought at a local pizza shop)

1¼ cups canola oil

½ cup sugar

If you're brave enough to say "goodbye," life will reward you with a new "hello"
—PAOLO COELHO

2018

In 2017, I finished high school and was set to leave for college in Washington, DC, in late August. My parents had always said that when I left for college, they would downsize. And just like any other child in denial, I didn't believe them. It was not until I packed my bags for college and lugged my suitcase down the stairs that I knew I was also saying goodbye to the house.

I remember feeling selfish and not wanting another family to live there after we moved. I didn't want other people making new memories in the place that had given me most of mine. I didn't want to drive past that house and know that someone else was roaming the rooms and halls as we once had. I hoped and prayed that, by some fated chance, we wouldn't have to sell it, and I would get to return to the house, but that was not in the cards.

When my parents first told me they had a likely buyer, I imagined the worst options. As it turns out, though, my grandmom had a few more tricks up her sleeve. Later, I discovered that sisters from St. Raphaela Center next door were buying our home to expand their retreat center. The place where my grandmother had lived for years was going to become a place for others to come and talk about life, love, and spirituality. The place where my grandmother dwelled would be a place of God now, just as she would have wanted. St. Raphaela's proximity was the main reason my grandmother wanted this house, and now it was getting a second life. It felt like everything had come full circle— as if she had it all planned from the beginning.

Many of the older Catholic sisters knew and loved my grandmother. In honor of her and one of her closest companions, Sister Philomena, they named our home the House of Hope. The same house that had given my family so much joy, love, and hope would now offer the same to others.

The sisters still welcome us to visit. I remember the first time I walked through the repurposed house; it had an entirely different vibration than before. Our formal living room was now a small chapel. The formal dining room, living room, pizza oven room, and sunroom were now rooms that held discussions, prayer, and reflection. Our bedrooms were converted to bedrooms for overnight retreatants and sisters. And our pool was made handicap accessible to be enjoyed by many, just as we had.

After the sisters transformed the house, I walked through each room for what felt like the first time. It felt holy; it felt whole. Since my grandparents passed, the spaces they occupied had felt half lived in, as if between two worlds. Now, those rooms are lived in once again. It is what my grandmother would have wanted.

The House of Hope gave my family so much, and it feels right to return that gift to the house. By writing about some of the most memorable moments we shared within those walls, I feel as if my grandmother's dream will forever be alive. As long as the house brings hope to others, my grandmother will be remembered and our memories will be preserved.

Following are recipes for some of the hors d'oeuvres we prepared for a housewarming party after the sisters took up residence.

SCALLOPS WRAPPED IN BACON *with* CALABRIAN AIOLI

Serves 6

INGREDIENTS

1.5 pounds thin-cut smoky bacon,
  cut into 2"–3" pieces

1 pound sea scallops
  (about 15 scallops to a pound)

¼ cup tamari or soy sauce

¼ cup dark-brown sugar

¼ cup orange juice

3 cups canola oil

2 tablespoons white wine vinegar

juice of **1** lemon

kosher salt, to taste

1 medium garlic clove, minced

3 tablespoons Calabrian chili
  peppers or sauce

equipment: toothpicks

PREPARATION

1. In a large bowl, stir together tamari, brown sugar, and orange juice. Add the scallops and toss them in the liquid mixture. Cover the bowl with plastic wrap and allow to chill for at least 45 minutes.

2. Prepare the aioli by adding the egg yolks to a food processor, and blend on high. Once the yolks have slightly thickened, add 1½ teaspoons of the vinegar. Continue to blend for another 2 minutes.

3. Slowly add about 1 cup of oil in a slow and steady stream. Next, add another 1½ teaspoons of vinegar and a fourth of the lemon juice. Alternate the addition of oil, vinegar, and lemon, in small increments. Be careful not to add the oil too quickly or the mixture will break. Process until the mixture turns a pale-yellow color.

4. Turn off the food processor and stir in the salt, pepper, and garlic. Transfer to a serving bowl, or a storage container if you are preparing it ahead of time.

5. Preheat oven to 425 degrees. Place a scallop at one end of a piece of bacon. Tightly wrap the bacon around the scallop and secure it with a toothpick. Transfer the package to a parchment-lined baking sheet. Continue until you have assembled all the scallops.

6. Bake 12–15 minutes, or until the bacon is cooked through. For extra-crispy bacon, broil for 2 additional minutes. Serve warm with the aioli on the side.

Pictured on page 98

MINI FILLET CROSTINI

PREPARATION

1. Combine tamari, garlic, ginger, and apple cider vinegar in a mixing bowl. Place the two pieces of beef into the bowl and turn the meat to coat. Cover with plastic wrap and refrigerate for 2 hours, or up to 24 hours.

2. Heat the olive oil in a large sauté pan over low heat. Add the onions and season with a few pinches of salt. Sauté slowly, stirring, until the onions caramelize, about 45 minutes. When the onions are reduced by half, add the balsamic vinegar and stir. Continue to cook and stir for 2–3 minutes. Set the onions aside.

3. Preheat the oven to 350 degrees.

4. Prepare the crostini by laying the slices of bread on a baking sheet. Brush each piece of bread with olive oil. Toast in the preheated oven 5–6 minutes or until toasted. The toasts can be premade and stored in an airtight container for up to 5 days.

5. Prepare the horseradish cream cheese spread by combining the cream cheese, horseradish, lemon zest, and salt and pepper in a mixing bowl. Set aside until ready to use. This can be stored in the refrigerator for up to 5 days.

5. Prepare the beef by transferring the marinaded meat to a baking dish. Pat the beef with paper towels. Sprinkle with salt and pepper.

6. Bake the fillet for about 22 minutes for rare doneness. Remove it from the oven and wrap the beef in aluminum foil. Let it rest at room temperature for 15 minutes. Place it in the refrigerator and allow the beef to cool completely.

7. When you are ready to assemble the crostini, transfer the beef to a cutting board and slice it thinly. Arrange the crostini on a large serving platter. Spread a teaspoon of the horseradish mixture on each slice. Top it with a piece of beef tenderloin, caramelized onions, and then some of the bell peppers, if desired. Serve this appetizer chilled.

Serves **6**

INGREDIENTS

2 8-ounce beef tenderloins

1 cup tamari or soy sauce

2 cloves garlic, finely minced

2 tablespoons fresh ginger, grated

¼ cup apple cider vinegar

2 tablespoons olive oil, and more for toasts

1 onion (Vidalia or other sweet yellow onion), thinly sliced

kosher salt, to taste

2 tablespoons aged balsamic vinegar

fresh Italian bread, baguette, sliced into ¼" slices

1 cup cream cheese

1½ horseradish, prepared

zest of **½** lemon

kosher salt and pepper, to taste

½ red or yellow pepper, finely diced (optional)

Rustic Focaccia Sandwiches

Serves 12

INGREDIENTS

1 sheet prepared focaccia
(recipe on page 63),
cut into 12 4" × 4" squares

GRILLED VEGETABLE FOCACCIA

PREPARATION

1. Brush the vegetables with olive oil and season with salt and pepper.

2. Arrange the vegetables on a grill over high heat. Grill each side for approximately 2 minutes per side. Transfer to a serving dish and allow the vegetable to cool.

3. Slice the grilled vegetables into 2" pieces. Slice 4 squares of focaccia bread in quarters lengthwise. Arrange the vegetables evenly among the 4 pieces of cut bread.

4. Top each slice with arugula and drizzle balsamic vinegar on top. Place the top piece of the focaccia on each slice and serve.

Grilled Vegetables

INGREDIENTS

1 medium eggplant, sliced, ¼" thick

2 medium zucchini, sliced ¼" thick

1 yellow squash, sliced ¼" thick

3 portobello mushrooms, cleaned and tops removed

4½ cups extra-virgin olive oil

kosher salt and pepper, to taste

6 ounces fresh mozzarella, sliced

balsamic vinegar, to drizzle

6 ounces fresh baby arugula

PROSCIUTTO FOCACCIA

PREPARATION

1. Slice 4 squares of focaccia bread in quarters lengthwise. Drizzle each piece with olive oil.

2. Layer the bread with 3 pieces of fresh mozzarella and then 2–3 pieces of prosciutto, creating ribbons rather than laying the prosciutto flat. Add the roasted red peppers as desired.

3. Top with arugula and another piece of bread. Serve.

Prosciutto

INGREDIENTS

¼ pound Prosciutto di Parma, thinly sliced

6 ounces fresh mozzarella, ½" slices

6 ounces roasted red peppers (previous recipe)

1 plum or beefsteak tomato, sliced

extra-virgin olive oil, to drizzle

4 ounces fresh baby arugula

TURKEY FOCACCIA

INGREDIENTS

8 ounces Carlino's house-roasted turkey breast

8 ounces roasted red peppers, prepared (recipe follows)

6 ounces fresh mozzarella, sliced

4 leaves romaine lettuce, cut into **4"** pieces

¼ cup pesto, prepared

Roasted Red Peppers

4 red bell peppers

2 yellow bell peppers

4 garlic cloves, minced

½ cup good-quality extra-virgin olive oil

salt and pepper, to taste

fresh Italian flat-leaf parsley, to taste

PREPARATION

1. Line a baking sheet with aluminum foil, add the peppers, and coat them with a thin layer of olive oil. Broil in the oven for about 15 minutes. The peppers should be charred and blistered. Flip the peppers over and broil for an additional 15 minutes.

2. Transfer the peppers to a brown paper bag and allow to cool. Then peel off the skin and discard the seeds.

3. Thinly slice the peppers and transfer them to a mixing bowl. Add olive oil, garlic, parsley, salt, and pepper. Set aside. The peppers can be stored in the refrigerator for up to 3 days. The olive oil will congeal when refrigerated. Allow the peppers to come to room temperature before serving.

ASSEMBLY

1. Slice 4 squares of focaccia bread in quarters lengthwise.

2. Spread the pesto on each side of the cut bread, then layer with the turkey breast, mozzarella, roasted red peppers, and romaine.

3. Place the bread top on each slice and serve.

It's a funny thing coming home. Nothing changes. Everything looks the same, feels the same, even smells the same. You realize what's changed is you.

—ERIC ROTH

2018–2021

The year we sold the house, our family started growing in different directions. I left for college in Washington, DC. Nick purchased his first home shortly after that. And Philip graduated from college and began his health journey. Two years later, Angela had her last child.

Angela is the COO of both of our stores. Nick is our chief of marketing. Philip is Angela's right-hand man and is actively working on healing his body through holistic medicine and food.

I recently graduated from college with a degree in psychology and a minor in anthropology. This book was my first postgraduation project, and I hope it is one of many future publications. I have also begun working full-time in our family business while attending graduate school, and I am proud to be a part of the future of our company.

My parents have talked about retiring ever since I began college. Yet, they are still active in the stores, working roughly seven days a week.

Sadly, in 2020 my grandfather passed away just before the pandemic arrived. I am so blessed to have been the last person to hold his hand and tell him that it was okay to go. We will forever be grateful for his legacy and the hardships he endured to give us the lives we have now.

As I was writing this book, a strange thing happened. On the way to work at the Ardmore market one morning, my mom and I discussed edits for the book and the recipes we would need to write. When we arrived at the store, one of our marketing team members told us that, when

he got to the office, he had found a random cookbook on the floor with pieces of paper scattered around it. We looked at the notes and recognized my grandmother's handwriting. The previous day, I had written her fiftieth-anniversary story, and it seems she had other ideas for

Pop (my grandfather) and I at a restaurant celebrating someone's anniversary.
Pop, Nicky, and our dog, Simba, playing T-ball in the backyard. This was our favorite pastime.

what to include. After looking at the recipes she had written and printed out a year before her death, I realized that they should be part of the book. It was a profound experience. My grandmother was always there when we needed her most.

We are constantly trying to achieve greater heights as a family and a business. We strive to ensure that our products are of the highest quality and locally sourced. We love to meet other immigrants like us who live their dreams and the dreams of those who came before them. There is much more coming in the future, and we hope you will follow us on social media to see what comes next. Our customers are the reason we do what we do. The following are recipes for some of our newer items and can be created at home or purchased in-store or online.

Thank you for coming along on this journey with us and for supporting my grandmother's dreams. While our House of Hope may no longer belong to us, it will never be forgotten for all it has contributed to our lives. I have learned through writing this book that what made our house a home was the people. Sometimes, home has a heartbeat, and ours certainly did.

I hope you will find your own House of Hope, and may you have the courage to begin again, whether in a new country far from home or a new venture in life. It is there that your House of Hope may lie.

KETO-FRIENDLY LASAGNA

PREPARATION

1. Preheat oven to 350 degrees.

2. On a parchment-lined baking sheet, add ⅓ of the Parmigiano-Reggiano in a thin layer covering the whole pan. Next, layer the eggplant slices on top of the cheese. Top with additional parmigiano cheese. Reserve some of the shredded cheese for the lasagna assembly.

2. Bake the eggplant-cheese layers for 10–15 minutes or until the cheese is melted and slightly crispy. Set aside to cool while you prepare the rest of the ingredients.

3. Lay out the remaining cut vegetables onto one or two baking sheets or platters. Brush each vegetable with olive oil and season with salt and pepper. Repeat on the other side.

4. Grill the vegetables until slightly charred, approximately 2 minutes per side. Set aside and allow the vegetables to cool.

5. Assemble the lasagna by adding about ½ cup of the prepared marinara on top of the eggplant layer and transfer to a 9" × 13" baking dish. You will have to cut the sheet to make it fit. Reserve the other pieces for another layer.

6. Layer the red or yellow bell peppers on the bottom of the dish, being sure to overlap them. Add a layer of the eggplant-and-cheese mix, piecing them together. Press down after placing each layer in place, using the palm of your hand.

7. Add the zucchini, overlapping the slices. Then add a light layer of marinara sauce, then peppers, then another layer of the sauce, until you use up all the vegetables.

8. Top the lasagna with a little more marinara sauce, the fresh basil leaves, and some of the reserved shredded Parmigiano-Reggiano. Bake approximately 20 minutes.

9. Cut the lasagna into squares and serve with warm marinara sauce on the side.

Serves 8

INGREDIENTS

1 cup Parmigiano-Reggiano

4 medium eggplant, peeled and sliced into ¼" pieces

3 red bell peppers, seeds removed, and cut into 3"–4" pieces

3 yellow bell peppers, seeds removed, and cut into 3"–4" pieces

3 medium zucchini, sliced about ¼" thick

2 medium yellow squash, sliced about ¼" thick

½ cup extra-virgin olive oil

kosher salt and pepper, to taste

marinara sauce, prepared

fresh basil leaves

STUFFED EGGPLANT

Serves 4

INGREDIENTS

2 large eggplants

2 cloves garlic, minced

½ large onion, diced

1 14.5-ounce can diced tomatoes

1 cup plain bread crumbs

1 cup ricotta cheese

2 tablespoons Locatelli cheese, plus extra for the top

¼ cup Italian flat-leaf parsley

2½ tablespoons olive oil, plus extra for cooking and drizzling on top

salt and black pepper to taste

PREPARATION

1. Preheat oven to 350 degrees and grease a baking sheet or line it with parchment paper.

2. Cut the eggplants in half lengthwise and scoop out the flesh so that mainly skin is left. Set aside the flesh.

1. Drizzle the hollowed eggplants with olive oil, sprinkle with some salt, and bake 15–20 minutes.

2. While the eggplants bake, chop the eggplant flesh and cook it in a large skillet with olive oil over medium heat. Add the garlic, bread crumbs, parsley, and salt and pepper. After 2 minutes, add the tomatoes.

3. Bring the mixture to a boil and reduce the heat. Cook for another 10 minutes and stir to ensure it doesn't stick or burn.

4. Fill the baked eggplant shell with the tomato mixture and add the ricotta atop each piece—enough to fill it out. Top with Locatelli cheese.

5. Spoon a layer of marinara sauce on the bottom of a large baking dish and place the stuffed eggplant on top of the sauce. Spoon 1–2 teaspoons of sauce on top of each eggplant. Bake for 25 minutes or until cooked thoroughly. Drizzle with extra-virgin olive oil, chopped parsley, and grated Locatelli cheese if desired. Serve warm.

DAIRY-FREE STUFFED BREAD

PREPARATION

Caponata Filling

1. Preheat oven to 425 degrees.

2. Halve the eggplant and salt both sides. Place it skin side down on an oiled baking sheet and bake for 15 minutes, then flip and bake for another 15–20 minutes or until tender.

3. When the eggplant is cool enough to handle, give it a rough chop. Add the olive oil and onion to a large skillet over medium heat. Sauté until the onion softens, and then add the chopped garlic.

3. Add the red peppers and salt and pepper and cook until tender. Add the eggplant and cook thoroughly, adding oil if necessary. Season to taste.

4. Add the tomatoes and some salt to the same pan, cooking until they break down. Add the capers and simmer for 25 minutes or until the mixture is thick and potent.

5. Add pine nuts, check seasonings, and remove from heat.

ASSEMBLY

1. Preheat oven to 375 degrees.

2. Press out the pizza dough with your hands and fingertips into a 10" circle. Put the caponata filling in the center. Fold opposing sides of the dough over the mixture and overlap them slightly, as if you're wrapping a gift. It's okay if some of the filling spills out the side.

3. If you wish, brush some olive oil onto the entire surface of the dough for color. Bake 20–25 minutes.

Serves 2-4

INGREDIENTS

1 pizza dough
(check for dairy-free ingredients)

1 large eggplant

3 tablespoons olive oil

1 small onion, chopped

3 garlic cloves, chopped

2 red peppers diced

salt and pepper to taste

1 28-ounce can crushed tomatoes

3½ tablespoons capers

2 tablespoons pine nuts

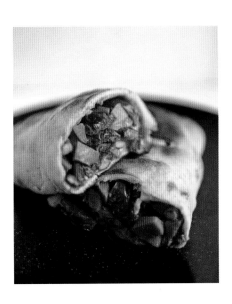

INDEX of RECIPES

NADIA CARLINO

is a graduate student at Drexel University.
The youngest member of the Carlino family, she has
written and given presentations about growing up
in the family business. When Nadia isn't writing
cookbooks, she writes poetry and fiction.

Designed by Danielle D. Farmer
Cover art by Cullen Hoppel, cullenhoppel.com

Type set in Hebden/Bodoni Terracina/Chaparral Pro

ISBN: 978-0-7643-6581-2
Printed in China

Published by Schiffer Publishing, Ltd.
4880 Lower Valley Road
Atglen, PA 19310
Phone: (610) 593-1777; Fax: (610) 593-2002
Email: Info@schifferbooks.com
Web: www.schifferbooks.com

For our complete selection of fine books on this and related subjects, please visit our website at www.schifferbooks.com. You may also write for a free catalog.

Schiffer Publishing's titles are available at special discounts for bulk purchases for sales promotions or premiums. Special editions, including personalized covers, corporate imprints, and excerpts, can be created in large quantities for special needs. For more information, contact the publisher.

We are always looking for people to write books on new and related subjects. If you have an idea for a book, please contact us at proposals@schifferbooks.com.

Other Schiffer Books on Related Subjects:

Secret Cities of Italy: 60 Charming Towns off the Beaten Path, Thomas Migge, ISBN 978-0-7643-6591-1

Secret Cities of Europe: 70 Charming Places Away from the Crowds, Henning Aubel, ISBN 978-0-7643-6289-7

Aroma Kitchen: Cooking with Essential Oils, Sabine Hönig and Ursula Kutschera, ISBN 978-0-7643-4793-1

FSC
www.fsc.org

MIX
Paper from responsible sources
FSC® C020560